"IT'S BEHAVIOUR, STUPID!"

WHAT REALLY DRIVES THE PERFORMANCE OF YOUR ORGANISATION

Steve Glowinkowski

This book is dedicated to the memory of my parents,
Beryl and Jozef Glowinkowski.

"It's behaviour, stupid!"
What really drives the performance of your organisation
Steve Glowinkowski PhD

Book Design and Setting by Neil Coe (neil@cartadesign.co.uk)
Set in Myriad Pro 10 on 13.5pt

First published in 2010 by;

Ecademy Press
6 Woodland Rise, Penryn, Cornwall UK TR10 8QD

info@ecademy-press.com
www.ecademy-press.com

Printed and Bound by;

Lightning Source in the UK and USA

Printed on acid-free paper from managed forests. This book is printed on demand, so no copies will be remaindered or pulped.

ISBN-978-1-905823-71-0

ACKNOWLEDGEMENTS

This book represents 25 years of research and practical consultancy experience. Throughout that time I have had the privilege of meeting and working with some exceptional leaders and managers. I have been continually and unabatedly supported by my wife, Margaret, and my family. I am immeasurably grateful to you all.

I have a fantastic team in my organisation who provide sterling support, encouragement and commitment and help create a Climate in which there is a continual striving to improve our performance to our clients.

I am especially appreciative and respectful to all of the clients with whom I have worked over the years. They have provided stimulus and challenge together with the fantastic opportunity to support their respective organisations. I must name three in particular for their ongoing provocation to advance the research and so deepen the degree of evidential proof that leaders' behaviours drive organisational performance. These are Richard Beaven, David Craggs and Helen Sweeney. Thank you!

No book like this is the sole endeavour of just one person. In particular, I owe an immense debt of gratitude to my colleague, David Physick, who has worked tirelessly in helping me to write and conceive what I hope is an exciting, practical and relevant manuscript.

Lastly, I must express my thanks to Mindy Gibbins-Klein, who has provided wise counsel throughout the past few months from conceiving the idea of writing a book to getting it published.

INTRODUCTION

The premise of this book is that a leader's behaviour or, rather, the quality of their leadership delivery, drives the performance of the group or business for which they are accountable. This is irrespective of the size or scope of the leadership challenge. It applies to the case of a supervisor of check-out staff; to the coach or captain of a cricket team; to the Head of a school or a Vice-Chancellor of a university; to the manager of a petro-chemical plant; or to a Chief Executive of a multi-national corporation. This statement is based upon research and management consultancy experience spanning over 25 years and involving the delivery of feedback in the context of leadership and career development with upwards of 20,000 managers.

These leaders have worked in an extremely large range of organisations, business sectors and geographical regions. This experience demonstrates that the leadership behaviours that drive performance are quantifiable and measurable. It is entirely feasible for individuals to raise their behavioural game in order to contribute more to their organisations and enable these enterprises to deliver better performance outcomes.

For those leaders to whom feedback has been provided as part of their quest to improve how they operate, it has been hugely important for them to know that they are receiving input that is based upon a rigorous methodology underpinned by sound, psychological rigour. In other words, "if you can't measure it, you can't change it." Leaders are kidding themselves if they think they can improve their performance by relying upon a process of measurement that is unsound by virtue of it being unreliably calibrated. In such instances, trying to benchmark oneself against 'the best' is an exercise in whimsy; it is unfeasible and impracticable.

The driving force for writing this book is to share this experience concerning how and why the behaviour of the manager specifically drives organisational performance. A clear and unambiguous insight into the causal link between different behaviours and performance outcomes will be provided. This is predicated in a clear and understandable framework beneath which lies an extensive and far-reaching methodology that has been established and continually expanded through ongoing research over the course of the past three decades. This book explains the broad and deep-reaching set of methodological principles that I have conceived and devised. **Above all, however, this is a practical book, but one based upon a robust foundation of valid research.**

There are very significant parallels between the economic conditions that prevail at the time of writing this book and those that existed at the outset of my consultancy career in the early 1980s when economic upheaval abounded. Businesses sought then to survive by 'down-sizing', 'de-layering' and 'off-shoring', all of which were deemed necessary by heightened competition in an intensifying, global business arena. Essentially, the critical impetus for organisations was achieving more with less.

This book is published at the time of another round of economic strain which some people, ranging from politicians to economists to business managers to media commentators, are suggesting is going to be the most serious for many decades. The shift of economic power appears to be moving from the occidental to the oriental. Interestingly, in the database of organisations with which my colleagues and I have worked, the most powerful 'measurement scores' ever achieved were by a Far Eastern business during the 1990s. Perhaps there is still more for the West to learn in terms of what constitutes this profile? This work, therefore, is timely and relevant to both the upswing and the downswing, and to the global community.

Unlike many other books that are littered with references to 'blue-chip' names, both organisational and individual, this is not the case in this body of work. This is not because my consultancy practice hasn't worked with the blue-chips, but rather because the nature of the work that is conducted involves dealing with some comprehensive, personal and psychological dynamics. It would be entirely unfair to those thousands of managers with whom my colleagues and I (the 'we' which I will use most frequently throughout the book) have worked to give any hint of breaching our sacrosanct confidentiality. Therefore, while many case studies are referenced, each is done so in a strictly anonymous manner. Suffice it to say, the range of enterprises with which we have worked ranges from the truly global to far smaller businesses, entrepreneurial start-ups, family businesses, healthcare institutions, religious orders and educational institutions, all operating in numerous socio-economic contexts.

Already, there have been references made to *psychology*, a term which tends to possess a strongly pejorative tenor for many people. However, no apology is made for its use because the science of psychology sits at the heart of what we do. How leaders and managers go about doing their work is entirely psychological. However, I do not intend to present an opaque, scientific or academic transcript before you. Neither do I intend to take an overtly light-hearted or frivolous approach. Being a leader or a manager is a serious responsibility to assume. Many other people (and their families) depend upon their boss's ability to set a course of direction for their enterprise and to win their hearts and minds to work hard and effectively to achieve the established goals. The application of the science of psychology, notably the specialist field of Organisational Psychology, is based upon a combination of research, management practice and consultancy delivery. I consider my work and that of my colleagues to be valid, practical and relevant to all shapes and sizes of organisations. I have sought to provide a fair balance of definitional explanation with some story-telling. A range of references is made to other books and articles, which are listed in an abridged bibliography at the end of the book.

Much has been written about the difference between what leaders and managers do (see John Kotter[1]). While I concur with many of the propounded views, throughout this book the terms are used interchangeably, not least for variety but also as valid labels representing any individual who has responsibility for the performance of other people.

In terms of whom this book is designed to be read by, I hope it will appeal to a wide spread of leaders from the most senior to those with a narrower remit. Of crucial importance is that the HR community will want to read the narrative. Most of all, I would like both these constituencies, i.e. business line managers and HR practitioners, to use the lexicon of the defined methodologies as a common language. Where, in those organisations with which we have worked, there is a truly collaborative approach between 'the line' and HR, some truly remarkable and positive transformations occur, particularly in terms of the *mood* that prevails in the organisation and the results that it achieves. 'Mood' is another of those pejorative words. None of my colleagues nor I subscribe to the concept of 'mood' meaning soft, benign or overtly friendly. We fully subscribe to the view that an economic candour must prevail in all organisations. Commercial businesses are there to make money for their owners (albeit fairly, equitably and lawfully); public sector and charitable enterprises are there to spend their funds wisely, efficiently and effectively. Each needs to seek to get the 'biggest bang for its buck'.

By 'mood' we actually mean 'Climate', a concept that has been around for many years (see Litwin and Stringer[2] from 1968, for instance) but very much reflects the *people dimension* of an organisation in terms of what they feel it is like to work there. 'Culture', which is a term used somewhat more frequently, relates to something entirely different. It concerns how things are done. **'Culture programmes' fail to generate improvement in organisational performance because, at best, they overlook the people dimension; at worst, they ignore it altogether.**

The title of this book posits that behaviour drives the performance of the organisation. The word 'behaviour' is used in two ways. Firstly, that the establishment of a great Climate causes everyone else in the organisation to deliver excellent behaviours. Secondly, that it is the behaviour of leaders and managers that creates the Climate in the first place. Great behaviour begets great behaviour. Ultimately, my colleagues and I are all 'behaviourists'.

Admittedly, much has been written previously about this subject, but I want the statistically underpinned analysis of the methodologies I explain to be regarded as 'a gale of creative destruction'[3] that cuts through the prevailing, unnecessary complexity and re-clarifies thinking in this arena. While Messrs Bower and Christensen[4] may have considered disruptive innovation in the field of technology, I see no reason why the same cannot be applied to the realm of leadership, management and organisational performance. Like the passage of a storm, I want this book to clear the air.

Quite bluntly, a far sharper and more concise understanding of the actual causation of organisational performance needs to be developed and applied by leaders and managers. Organisations need to perform better; the economic gains to be achieved are undoubted; more importantly, there are immense socio-economic benefits available as well.

Each chapter is designed to be self-contained in terms of providing a full and clear explanation of that area of the methodology. In summary, the chapters of the book address the following themes:

- Chapter 1 focuses on 'performance'. It is essential that there is a common sense of understanding about what this term means so it is considered from a range of perspectives and angles. In the commercial sector does this just mean raw profitability or something else, e.g. growth, market share etc? In the social sector, e.g. in education, does performance simply concern exam results or is it also relevant to include some social aspiration, such as reducing the incidence of teenage pregnancies or lowering truancy through creating a learning environment in which kids wish to participate? From the point of view of individual employees, their attitude towards reward, development and promotion is considered. In reality, performance is the ultimate outcome of what the entity - be it company, hospital, university or individual - has set out to achieve in terms of its purpose and objectives.

- In the second chapter the foundational framework, called the

Glowinkowski Integrated Framework, is explained. This clearly shows how bosses, through their behaviour, create a Climate which, in turn, drives the performance of the organisation they manage by fundamentally impacting the behaviour of the people for whom they are accountable.

- The third chapter explains the concept of the 'Leadership Dynamic', which helps shape Climate. What is it that bosses do in terms of their behaviours, the structure of the organisation they set in place and the manner in which they govern crucial processes that affects the quality of Climate? Do they build a Climate where high performance is sought by everyone or one where mediocrity prevails? The linkages between these levers of the Leadership Dynamic and Climate are explored to help you focus your attention on those drivers that are going to have the most impact on your organisation's performance.

- The fourth chapter examines the concept of competencies and seeks to reawaken awareness to the purity of the original foundational research (see Richard Boyatzis[5]), namely that competencies are behavioural; they do not encapsulate other factors such as personality, skills, knowledge or values. Indisputably, it is behavioural competencies that differentiate an outstanding from an average performer.

- Chapter 5 explores the territory of personality by considering the question, "Why do we do what we do?" Our approach to analysing personality in terms of 'Predispositions', i.e. preferred or natural behaviours and motivations, is explored in depth. From an organisational perspective, 'personality sucks'. This is because organisations require people to deliver certain specific behaviours rather than their underlying personality.

- Chapter 6, therefore, considers the influential links between aspects of personality, as viewed through the lens of predispositions and motivations, and actual delivered behaviour. In other words, "If I am 'wired up' in such a way, how am I likely to behave? What is actually needed, given the contextual circumstances in which my organisation operates? If my personality does not match this, what can I do to operate or behave differently?"

- Chapter 7 provides an array of case studies that present greater and more specific detail than in the examples and anecdotes that feature throughout the earlier chapters. As remarked earlier, these are entirely anonymous but nevertheless demonstrate the efficacy of our work. These case studies demonstrate the measurable performance improvements that occurred as a result of the positive shift in leaders' behaviours in the various management groups with which we worked.

- Chapter 8 outlines how all this theory can be made practical. After all, Kurt Lewin, the US psychologist regarded as one of the founding fathers in the field of Organisational Psychology, said, "There is nothing so practical as a good theory"[6]. A range of possible approaches is described that will help embed our methodologies into organisational life. From an economic perspective, our approach does not leave a legacy of a massive, perpetual drain on costs through ongoing consultancy fees. Paraphrasing the words of an ancient Chinese proverb, "Give a man a fish and he will eat for a day. Teach a man to fish and he will eat for the rest of his life." Our approach is to teach.

- Chapter 9 provides a summary of all that the book contains in an attempt, if you wish, to provide a quick reference guide.

This book contains quite a lot of definitional content. I encourage you to take the time to read through this and absorb it, particularly through reflecting how each element relates to you and the organisational situation in which you work. This content is interspersed with a variety of anecdotal commentary and case study examples which, hopefully, makes it easier for you to 'apply' the definitional context to your own situation.

Throughout the book, I use the terms 'he' or 'his' when describing different situations. By no means is this to be construed as gender specific; it is to be read as embracing both genders. I consider it preferable to use this form rather than the plural 'them' or 'their' or the somewhat awkward 'he/she', 'him/her' or 'his/hers'.

I make some quite direct, possibly contentious commentary for which I make no apology. There are too many books that try to appease all quarters. I have a view and I have chosen to express it forthrightly and candidly. Whether you agree or disagree, let me know by writing to us at itsbehaviourstupid@glowinkowksi.com.

I want you to enjoy this book and for it to have a transformational impact upon how you rate what you do as a leader or manager and to stimulate you to raise your game by improving your performance contribution to your organisation. I do not seek to entertain but to educate and I hope I have succeeded.

Finally, why is the book titled as it is? At the time of writing, a US presidential election was taking place and the famous phrase, "It's the economy, stupid", which was used by Bill Clinton in his 1992 campaign has been recalled by many commentators. I have adapted this to reflect the absolute nub of my research and consultancy experience, i.e. that it is managers' behaviours, more than any other attribute that they bring with them to their role, which will distinguish their performance as good, bad or indifferent. Quite simply, "It's behaviour, stupid!"

Dr. Steve Glowinkowski

BIOGRAPHY

Steve Glowinkowski, BSc (Hons), MA, PhD, C.Psychol, FRSA

Steve's early academic career was in the fields of organisational psychology, management and statistics. Steve is a Chartered Psychologist and a Fellow of the Royal Society of Arts.

Steve's commercial background involved over ten years' experience in a series of internal consultancy, managerial and Director roles within the chemical industry and the financial services sector. The majority of this work related to the delivery of major organisational change, the development of organisation-specific behavioural competency frameworks and their subsequent implementation within a leadership and talent management context. In this period, Steve worked extensively in North and South America, Asia, Australia, South Africa and Europe.

In the early 1990s, Steve established Glowinkowski International. This would operate in both the research and consultancy fields. The former would produce bespoke intellectual property, which could then be applied through consultancy activities in the areas of leadership behaviour, culture change and organisational performance improvement. Since founding the business, Steve has built up the reach of the organisation, which now works with a wide range of international organisations across a variety of sectors. These extend from global conglomerates to small, entrepreneurial start-ups, from major public sector entities to smaller organisations operating within the voluntary sector.

As a consultant, Steve has had extensive involvement in the assessment and development of senior managers and executive directors. He has also conducted extensive research into the question of what differentiates outstanding performance at the level of the individual, a team, a business function and an entire organisation. This research has led to the formulation of a cohesive set of methodologies, which have been implemented within numerous international organisations.

INDEX

CHAPTER I:

What do we mean by performance?

How many times have you heard the phrase, "Our people are our most important asset" uttered by senior leaders? Often dismissed as cliché or flimsy, rhetorical comment, it is, in fact, the greatest truth in organisational management. The essence of this book seeks to demonstrate that truth by showing how organisations that maximise the skills, talents and innovative capabilities of individuals and the teams they form deliver outstanding performance. The absolute premise of this book is that it is bosses' behaviour or, rather, their quality of leadership delivery, which drives the performance of the group or business for which they are accountable. This is achieved by their building and sustaining an environment which we call 'Climate', in which people can flourish and operate at their fullest potential. Accordingly, therefore, the fundamental view in today's global economy is that it is the *people dimension* that provides the sustainable differentiator in terms of organisational performance, be it an organisation operating as a commercial enterprise or one existing in the 'not-for-profit' sector.

Without getting too deeply immersed in philosophical semantics, the following question needs answering:

> *"What is meant by the term 'performance'; what is it precisely and what do the different people involved in organisations expect as a result of how it performs?"*

The first chapter explores this concept of organisational performance in both public and private sector organisations. It also contemplates the issue from the perspectives of the different individuals, teams or stakeholder groups that give rise to the organisation's existence; for instance:

- owners, shareholders, trustees etc.

- senior management

- employees

- customers

- the community in which the organisation operates.

These groups may not always possess congruent expectations. Additionally, there is the potential for further friction within the groups themselves because different managers or teams may have expectations and aspirations that do not sit comfortably with each other.

What is organisational performance?

It is probably not unfair to say that many people now think performance is a linear measurement relating to financial performance. In the business community of profit-making organisations, this is profit (although even here there are different calibrations that are applied). In the non-profit making sector, simplistically it concerns 'meeting budget'.

Increasingly, this mono-dimensional view is being challenged by the concept of 'Corporate Social Responsibility', although the economist Milton Friedman[7] wrote in 1970 that, "The social responsibility of business is to increase its profits". The debate forged by this article has not abated. If anything, it has intensified, particularly around the issue of the scale of profit being reported by the very largest organisations.

What about duration, tenure or longevity as measures of success? A business that has been around for a while is likely to know its markets' ebbs and flows. Or does it? It is not the business, the organisation *per se*, that knows this; rather, it is its people that have this acumen.

However, continuing with the question of time as a moniker of success, it is not unreasonable to ask the following question, "Which are the more successful organisations?"

- Relatively recent incarnations such as Apple or Amazon; or

- UK banks such as Barclays or Lloyds TSB, which both claim 300 plus years' of continuous existence; or slightly more esoterically

- Zildjian, which has manufactured cymbals for almost 400 years since its formation in Constantinople; or even

- Aberdeen Harbour in Scotland which is reputed to be the UK's oldest business, trading since 1136.

In the UK, the FTSE 100 index of the country's largest corporations comprises of many companies with less than 50 years' history; the world's largest bank in the 1950s was Midland Bank but this has been subsumed into HSBC and its brand no longer exists. In the US, Richard Foster and Sarah Kaplan[8] speculated that by 2020, 75% of the S&P 500 will comprise companies not known at the turn of the millennium.

Away from longevity and the traditional measure of profit are concepts such as Economic Value Added[9] and Value Based Management (VBM)[10]. This latter approach to financial management is much more invasive to the way the organisation is managed; indeed, it demands a complete cultural change. Successful implementation of VBM demands explicit commitment throughout the organisation to generating greater shareholder value. Training is a vital ingredient. Giving managers the accountability to drive their business unit's performance, albeit congruent with overarching corporate strategy, is another crucial component. Vitally, it is about keeping things simple because it is all too easy to overawe the concept with a myriad of financial rules. This requires clear linkage of strategic planning, budgeting and the goals of individuals' performance plans.

One article about VBM was headlined, "Power profitability with value-based management – *if* you focus just 20% on the numbers/80% on the people" [11]. So, as we countered just before, it is the people dimension, more than anything else, which makes the difference to a company's performance.

Measuring business performance

The ultimate yardstick, however, for measuring performance remains financial.

For owners of businesses, be they majority owners or individual investors, the question of profit performance remains critical. Essentially, each considers the following assessment of risk:

> *"Does the potential return reflect a good margin above the risk-free return I could get from alternative investments and above that available for the same level of risk I can achieve elsewhere?"*

A business' financial performance can be measured in a number of ways, for example:

- Profit, e.g. EBITDA (earnings before interest, tax, dividends and amortisation)

- Profit growth over a given period

- Share price performance over a given period

- EPS (Earnings per share) growth versus market/competitors

- Dividend yield over a given period of time

- Rate of return on capital (risk adjusted or not)

- Economic Value Added (EVA)

- Total shareholder return (a precept of VBM).

It is increasingly common to see these financial metrics as the main drivers of senior executives' remuneration schemes. Sometimes, but not always, they also drive the remuneration of other people in the organisation. It is not, of course, the organisation that defines the thresholds of 'good performance'. This is done by individuals, e.g. a remuneration committee in larger organisations, owner-managers in smaller enterprises. The consequences of these decisions upon others in the organisation cannot and should not be under-estimated. In my own work with organisations, I have frequently heard groups of employees saying, "The senior management team is driven only by bonuses". This often has a corrosive effect, not just across that internal, employee stakeholder community but over other external groups, too.

Generally, the question of remuneration appears to be a hot topic across all types of organisation - commercial and not-for-profit - with the flames fanned by the media's coining of the pejorative epithet 'fat-cat'. This is even more barbed where bonus paid and performance achieved appears to have little correlation. Fifteen years ago, Alfie Kohn[12] generated a vigorous debate following publication of a book and associated articles about the efficacy of incentive schemes. In this, in answering his own question, "Do rewards motivate people?" he responded, "Absolutely. They motivate people to get rewards." How prescient was this comment as I write this during the banking crisis of 2008!

Perhaps it is easier to conjecture acceptance for massive financial rewards when economic conditions are rosy but, in a recession when organisational survival is paramount, is paying very high rewards still viable? Getting more from less becomes not just an objective but the single-most vital imperative. Should leaders be rewarded for eliminating many jobs from an organisation in order to help it survive? Perhaps the other side of the coin needs to be considered? The question then becomes, "What has an organisation's leadership done, or not done, that has resulted in it getting into such a predicament?" Does that merit reward?

My work in the manufacturing sector during the late 1970s and early 1980s was driven from the perspective of 'getting more from less'. This meant ensuring that a factory with 300 employees could deliver the same, if not better, output with a 25% reduction in staff.

Since then, the massive bound in technological capability, which firstly enabled the globalisation of production and service, continues to fuel the drive for productivity. Through the late eighties, nineties and up until about 2006, it was not recession-driven survival that impelled the search for greater efficiency but aggressive competition. Out of this competitive vortex has arisen the need for organisations to acquire and retain the best people. This phenomenon enjoys its own academic, now wider journalistic, epithet, namely 'the war on talent'[13]. An organisation perceived by its own people to be in difficulty often haemorrhages its most capable people unless their loyalty has been won by its leaders (note the deliberate use of the word 'won', rather than 'bought').

In a rising, optimistic market, the focus shifts towards growth, delivered organically and by the acquisition of other enterprises. One consistent thread has been the impact of technology, where the time taken to get new products from design to the shelf has been much reduced. I remember a conversation with a designer in the automotive industry who remarked that when he started work the time period taken for a new design to get from the drawing board to the road was measured in years. Now it is measured in months and the variety of models within a particular range is significantly greater, too.

Some organisations I have dealt with have positioned new product development at the heart of their strategy, e.g. establishing a goal to derive a significant proportion of revenue from products under two years old because they derive healthier margins[14].

While in both downbeat and upbeat market conditions, the leaders' concentration remains firmly cast on improving profit (or, perhaps, reducing loss in the former circumstance), what is required in each, very different, market condition is a different set of managerial capabilities. These capabilities cover a range of managerial attributes, i.e. their skills, knowledge and experience, their behavioural competencies, their values and beliefs. The relative importance of this range of qualities is driven by the economic context. The recession calls for managers to be able to get the most out of things, i.e. driving excellence, hitting deadlines, managing tight budgets; the latter growth mode calls for different characteristics such as perceptive innovation, acuity of new ideas, and knowledge development.

In Messrs Kaplan and Norton's seminal work concerning the Balanced Scorecard[15], they consider what else needs to be measured other than bottom line performance, be that profit or adherence to funding budget, which is affected by many causal factors. These include employee and customer satisfaction (although I accept that some people may argue that the organisation that focuses solely on creating happy workers and/or customers may not actually be financially viable). In a bank, the desire to measure leadership proficiency and effectiveness resulted in my commencing working with it (and meeting my colleague David who helped me write this book). The nub of this important work is to measure cause and effect; indisputably, a critical causation of strong organisational performance is the quality of its leadership. This is what we measure and diagnose and which I go on to describe in later chapters.

An additional range of measures probes deeper into the mechanics and functional aspects of a business, and includes:

- Sales performance, e.g. growth over a given period, growth versus market/competitors

- Market share, e.g. is its trend growing or declining, is the market itself growing or declining?

- Market rating, e.g. credit risk rating strengthens or weakens access to affordable capital to fund expansion (perhaps by acquisition)

- Quality, e.g. brand perception, customer service satisfaction

- Staff satisfaction, e.g. number of people wanting to work for the organisation, ease of filling vacancies

- Safety, e.g. days since last accident/incident

- Efficiency and/or productivity

- Regulatory compliance

- Favourable PR commentary

- Regarded as the 'bellwether' for the sector

- New product development, e.g. first-mover or emulator, speed to market

- Environmental regard, e.g. 'green' credentials

- Corporate Social Responsibility.

Across this admittedly non-exhaustive list of factors there plays an array of political, economic, social, technological and environmental factors. Most businesses are affected by these factors but some extremely large organisations including oil companies, banks, pharmaceuticals and IT, actually shape the dynamics themselves.

Regulation has affected how businesses operate. For instance, the governance of safety to improve working conditions in heavy industry is far more prominent now than it was 20 years ago. Specifically, in my experience, the attention paid to safety in the rail and construction industries is now extremely high. In the former, any critical incidence gives rise to a great deal of hand-wringing in the media about profit being put before safety since privatisation.

The scrutiny of the media, made instantaneous by the internet and 24/7 news channels, has had a considerable impact upon how organisations operate. Across a range of sectors from mineral extraction to manufacturing e.g. producing clothing apparel for leading retailers, the consequences of video footage being posted on the internet showing poor working conditions (mainly in the third world) can have significant, adverse PR consequences. Millions spent marketing an image of being a 'caring corporate citizen' can be undermined in a flash.

Performance in the not-for-profit sector

In the UK, many people work in organisations where profit is fundamentally not the key measure of performance, e.g. the UK's largest organisation is the National Health Service. From the list of metrics just provided, many - and certainly profitability - appear less relevant. Or are they?

In terms of the types of organisations we are considering, we include educational institutions, e.g. primary and secondary schools, and universities; hospitals, Primary Care Trusts and the ambulance service; social service departments, e.g. child welfare, the probation service; the military; the police; the fire service; charitable organisations; religious orders etc. However, these organisations still exist for a purpose and to deliver some form of performance outcome; for example:

- In education, the performance outcome focus has, more recently, been singularly targeted on to the academic achievement of the students, with the result that the clamour for places at 'high performing schools' is strenuous. At a more basic level, however, some schools exist in very difficult, socially challenging communities. Here, a key performance outcome might be, firstly, to increase attendance and reduce truancy. Efforts may be expended to lower the incidence of teenage pregnancies, or alcohol or drug abuse, or involvement in social disorder or other forms of crime.

At one school, with which we have worked, based in an extremely deprived area of a major city, the new Head recognised that attempts to win specialist status in more academic disciplines were not appropriate for her *clients*. "The children here want to be pop stars, celebrities." Her school applied and won specialist status as an Arts and Drama College. The effect on the pupils' attitude in terms of seeing relevance for what the school could provide was palpable. They became genuinely interested in science: physics informed them about the body's leverage mechanisms – rather helpful in dance; biology informed them about diet, nutrition and breathing - all important in performance; and geography - African music heavily influences modern musical genres.

- For universities, the introduction of fees potentially gives rise to a change of attitude towards 'quality', both in terms of academic, e.g. good teaching standards, and pastoral provision, e.g. high standards of accommodation, access to ICT and leisure and sports facilities.

For one senior leader of a University, with which we work, the phrase 'not-for-profit' is something of an anathema: "If I don't make a profit, how do I invest for the future and attract talent to help manage the University and deliver a great experience to my customers, the students?" he asks.

In these two examples, it is interesting to see that the two high-performing leaders consider that they have customers. Such contextualisation is not common-place in our experience.

- In the health sector, enforced performance drivers, e.g. speed of delivery of care, is jarring with the value systems of many people who operate and run these types of organisations an argument prevails for drivers to focus upon outcomes not outputs, i.e. the quality of clinical care, recovery rates, lowering re-infection rates. These can be construed as proxies for the 'rate of return' measures that prevail in commercial organisations (it is a form of systems thinking[16]).

- Social services organisations are driven to improve the well-being of disadvantaged people living in the locality in which they operate.

- For the police service, their performance is measured in terms of response times, crimes solved, convictions, public order.

- Charitable organisations tend to have a core interest for which they seek to raise funds and then distribute these in the most effective way (this has come under closer scrutiny of late).

I could, of course, go on; however, the key point is that **all** organisations have performance outcomes upon which they need to focus, whether these are imposed by mandate upon them or are more optional. In this sense, therefore, whatever is/ are the (chosen) outcome(s) is what we mean by 'organisational performance'.

Internal functional expectations

So, depending upon the organisation's primary external focus and over-arching performance objectives, supporting performance measures are also needed to cover internal functional objectives within the overall organisation:

- Marketing – impact in terms of brand recognition, identity and reputation; sales generated; in terms of 'below the line' advertising, what response rate is engendered. For marketing to set itself such performance markers, the famous remark allegedly made by Lord Leverhulme in the early part of the 20th century should not be forgotten, namely, "I know half my marketing works but, unfortunately, I don't know which half."

- IT – reliability, efficiency, modernity, usability (banks, for instance, target the 'up-time' of critical systems, e.g. cash dispensers [ATMs]).

- Human Resources – effectiveness of staff recruitment, policies to retain and grow the capability of the workforce.

As mentioned before, organisations do not themselves make the decisions to determine their performance intentions. That, usually, is the role of the senior managers, e.g. Board of Directors, Board of Governors, Board of Trustees etc.[17] as emphasised by Bob Garrett and Adrian Davies who, effectively, are making behaviourally-biased arguments. These corporate bodies comprise individuals; it is through their cognition more than anything else that institutional goals are set. Essentially, the onus on this group of organisational representatives is to strive to improve the organisation's overall performance, however that is defined and measured. How this is done and by whom is a critical determinant of what can ultimately be achieved.

In most organisations, it is usually senior management that is the only group to articulate an organisation's objectives because they (are expected to) possess a clearer, more detailed understanding of the implications of their intentions. However, someone like Ricardo Semler[18] may disagree. Indeed, one of our clients during the late 1990s - a business unit in a major bank - devolved target-setting to a cross-functional, multi-level team. (This business was still strongly unionised and operated in a region of the UK known for its poor management/union relations.) This group actually set more exacting goals than the management team felt were viable and, because the targets were set in this exceptionally strong inclusive manner, staff readily accepted them and subsequently delivered performance in excess of them!

Therefore, in more enlightened managerial teams, a great deal of 'understanding the possible' is built up by virtue of the extent to which they seek input and counsel from those their decisions will affect, e.g. customers, staff, local community etc. Although the managers determine the final decisions, the process is founded on two-way collaboration. Critically, a CEO's and their Directors' priority challenge and task, whether in a profit-making business or a non-profit making organisation, is to win the explicit, not just tacit, agreement from other stakeholders to their plans. It is against these plans that the leaders' and managers' performance should be measured, assessed and rewarded. <u>Failure should not be rewarded.</u>

These high-level goals then need to be expanded and cascaded across the organisation by subsidiary, function, department, team and individual so that there is supportive alignment and congruence. For example, setting out to achieve a holistic cost/income ratio dictates certain efficiency expectations. At a practical level, this may concern protocols about style or class of transport and accommodation used by people travelling during the course of their work (there are many apocryphal stories about Sam Walton's (who founded Wal-Mart) expectations of his managers, e.g. sharing motel rooms to reduce cost). At a more complex level, this may concern reducing wastage and re-work arising from production or service inefficiencies. Recent outsourcing of Contact Centres hasn't necessarily wrought the financial gains that organisations expected. While each individual call may be cheaper, the fact it may take five or six calls for a customer to get his issue sorted destroys the projected economic gains.

So, having planned and decided on what it wants to achieve, how does management increase its probability of success in hitting its established goals? At this point, I encourage you to consider how your organisation establishes its goals and how it goes about achieving them - assuming, of course, that it does!

There is a single path through this minefield. It is, as I stated at the beginning of this chapter, through the organisation's people. General Patton expressed this succinctly by saying, "Tell your people what you want to be done, but not how". From CEO to the most junior person in the organisation, there must be clarity about what the organisation's goals are and an understanding about how each person contributes to these objectives through what they do.

In the 1960s, Bill Shankly at Liverpool Football Club set out to create the world's best football team (or, as he put it, a 'bastion of invincibility')[19]. Not only did the players appreciate what they had to do but the ground-staff understood their role, too, creating what was regarded at the time as the best playing surface (pitch) in the UK, which conferred an advantage for the home team.

The first and foremost responsibility of an organisation's management is, without doubt, to create this type of 'high performance *climate*', such as Shankly created. At this point, consider what you regard as the components of great climate. (We shall return to this concept in much more depth in a later chapter.)

What is *performance* from the individual's perspective?

The previous sections considered performance from the perspective of the overall goals of the organisation and internal functions. It is clear that whilst there may be a range of different performance criteria established, there is one thing that is common, which is the absolute need to align and develop the right performance climate for the desired business outcome. However, what about the individual outside the upper echelons of management? What do they feel about performance? What do they want? What's in it for them? Until this is understood by managers, it is impossible for them to create a high-performance climate.

The following anecdote illustrates the two contrasting faces of attitude towards corporate performance and individual reward.

Reward

Consultants were involved in facilitating two workshops within days of each other. At the first, involving a group of industrial physicists, i.e. scientists working within a commercial enterprise rather than in an academic research environment, their key focus on performance concerned maintaining funding for their research and for their research to be regarded as relevant and objective by their peers in terms of certain scientific parameters. That they successfully introduced a number of innovations that wrought commercial benefit for their organisation was of less concern. At the second workshop involving a team of investment bankers, it was clear that one was upset at the level of his annual bonus compared to that of a colleague in light of his perception about the amount of business they had both won for the bank. Interestingly different perspectives on corporate performance and personal reward!

What does motivate people? Probably the first framework to enter our consciousness was Abraham Maslow's 'hierarchy of needs'[20]. Maslow's model simply states that motivational sets are represented in a hierarchy. At the bottom of the hierarchy, there are basic needs such as hunger, thirst, security and safety. Until these are satisfied, an individual's motives are fairly basic and focused on bottom-line survival. However, once these become satisfied, Maslow argued that people move into a higher order of need, namely social needs, self-esteem, and eventually ascending to the highest level of self-actualisation. Certain rudimentary issues need to be satisfied before individuals feel able to reward themselves. Consider the following illustration.

The seat-belt sign is illuminated

Picture yourself seated on an airplane, waiting to take off. As the plane taxis down the runway your motivation is likely to be at the bottom of the pyramid, i.e. you are thinking "will we take-off safely and successfully?". Once airborne and cruising at 35,000 feet, your ego demands that you are well looked after and a drink and watching a movie on the in-flight entertainment system takes care of that. For some, they will use the time the flight provides to read something interesting and stimulating to expand their field of knowledge. Suddenly, the plane hits an air pocket, drops dramatically, and your drink is in your lap, the film is stopped and the book is dropped on to the floor. Safety becomes your primary concern. But, calm is restored and, gradually, higher order motivators take over as you start to read again and ask for a replacement drink.

In a vein similar to Maslow is Frederick Herzberg's[21] two-factor theory of motivation. The first set of motivators is termed 'satisfiers' and equates to Maslow's lower order, embracing things such as hygiene, safety, pay and the general conditions of the workplace. People need to feel these are being met before they give any consideration to the second set of motivators, called 'motivators'. When first reported in the 1960s, Herzberg remarked, "Forget praise. Forget punishment. Forget cash. Make their jobs more interesting instead." These fundamental, intrinsic qualities of an individual's role are the most crucial for excellent performance to occur. Extrinsic reward comes a distinct second.

Our study of motivation

From research, I have sought to assess the relative balance of intrinsic, i.e. what the job itself provides, and extrinsic, i.e. financial reward and motivation in terms of the respective levels of importance to the individual. Over the last couple of years, over 500 senior managers, primarily based in Europe and South Africa, have been surveyed via questionnaire. The essential message is that if you measure, as it were, the 'cut of the pie', I have observed that, on average, this senior management population's desire for intrinsic motivation accounts for about 60% of the variation, compared to a 40% need for extrinsic motivation.

This indicates this group's relatively stronger importance for more of the intrinsic type factors in their work, e.g. the need for challenge, autonomy and fulfilment, rather than the extrinsic motivators of money and reward. That there is 40% aggregate need for the extrinsic illustrates that money and reward are not unimportant. Herzberg argued they are a fundamental threshold requirement. In this sense, while money is important it is, however, secondary to the more intrinsic needs of, to use Maslow's terminology, 'self-actualisation' to which people aspire.

This type of research has tended to be conducted with relatively senior management groups, but we have also done exhaustive surveys throughout organisational structures down to the most junior levels. Quite recently, I conducted a qualitative focus group process involving over 450 clerical and administration staff from a financial services organisation in the UK.

In these workshops, individuals were given four sets of questions which included:

- What do you see as the key issues that need to be addressed by this organisation?

- How do you perceive the leadership style in this organisation?

- If you could make three changes in the company what would they be?

- What would you keep the same – what's good about this organisation? (provide three examples)

These questions were put to groups of up to about 20 people. Individuals worked in pairs and brain-stormed their responses to each question. Individuals were allowed as much time as they needed and, following their work on each question, the workshop facilitator simply collated their responses on flip chart. Prior to the workshop, individuals were assured absolute confidentially/anonymity as to their responses. The idea was to present the aggregated response to both themselves and also senior management groupings as a whole.

To the question, "What changes would you make?", over 90% of responses related to the need for greater focus of direction, the need for more effective team working, and the need to receive more effective feedback in appraisals. Furthermore, these employees wanted to see a clear differential 'link' between reward and actual performance and contribution.

It was obvious that none of the desired changes were directly linked to introducing higher levels of pay and improving conditions. Indeed, the vast majority of requirements related to improving the effectiveness of the company's operational practices and how, as a result, such improvements would enable people to give their best in their jobs. When asked, "What would you not want to change in the company?" people tended to focus on the quality of interpersonal relationships and the general atmosphere that prevails.

This work in the motivational area clearly indicates individuals within organisations to be predominantly motivated by factors other than straight-forward reward. Indeed, it may be that when people are motivated by reward it is more about the power and status that reward can confer rather than reward in the Maslow or Herzberg context. Also, given their personal fulfilment drivers, it is important to recognise that the results can be highly variable depending upon the group in question.

Teams

Over the last 25 years and around the world, my colleagues and I have conducted numerous team-based workshops. Whilst it would be wrong to say that precisely the same drivers of performance exist for a CEO, the members of the Board of Directors and the Executive Management committee as for more junior levels, it is nevertheless clear that such people are driven by the need to have the opportunity to do an effective job in terms of *what they understand their organisation is aiming to achieve*. This is the fundamental genome of a high-performance Climate.

In essence, people really enjoy the opportunity to do a damned good job.

In most organisations, people work in business units, functions, departments and teams. Bruce Tuckman (1965)[22] conceived the concept of teams: *forming, storming, norming, performing and adjourning*. Teams are not only, and should not be regarded as, groups of people assembled for some organisational convenience. Over groups, teams have advantages of working towards common goals and understanding how their different roles and responsibilities integrate with each other. Team games, e.g. American football, highlight this by identifying the common goal to win, combined with appreciation of how 'offence' and 'defence' must work in a co-ordinated manner to achieve the overarching aim.

Groups often tend to be affected with in-fighting arising from one person trying to impose his opinion on the others. When this goes too far, and people acquiesce to that individual, cults emerge which have less than edifying characteristics. In teams, differences of opinion are valued and how these are resolved effectively is understood. We hear people talking of teams possessing an '*esprit de corps*', a real sense of inclusion and involvement in determining its destiny. In order to achieve its sense of intent or purpose, the team possesses a sense of honesty that enables members to provide supportive, challenging feedback to each other, bolstering known strengths and providing a platform for mutual support to address identified weaknesses. Teams can change their composition and performance; indeed this changing constituency enables them to achieve more, more quickly. This gives a team a flexibility that an ordinary group cannot hope to possess due to rigidity, which is caused by people sticking to their guns, their roles and reward systems. Performance, therefore, is a collective experience, not bound by structures and rules but by shared purpose and objective.

So far, performance has been considered 'from the inside looking out' but it is also important to consider what other external stakeholders expect of the organisation with which they are associated.

Customer expectations

When we mentioned Universities, I remarked about their need to change their thinking about the quality of service delivered because of the likely change of expectation in the minds of students brought about by the introduction of fees in England. The students or, rather, the 'customers' of these institutions may begin to expect 'more bang for their buck'. In the litigious US, lawsuits for failure to deliver value brought by student customers against their University or college are not uncommon and the same may become prevalent in England. Whatever, it does highlight that customers have their own perceptions of organisational performance.

In terms of customers measuring organisational performance, the domain is filled by research organisations conducting quantitative and qualitative assessment, but on behalf of the supplying enterprise more so than the customer. However, nothing beats the highly visible explicit action of customers in terms of their flocking to or abandoning organisations. In the academic world, the seminal article to provide a measurement calibration was provided by Parasuraman and others back in 1991[23], in which they identified five critical dimensions of service, namely:

- Reliability - people do what they promise

- Assurance - people are knowledgeable and convey this

- Tangibles - people (leaders) provide good quality facilities and people (to serve the organisation's customers)

- Empathy - people are caring and give individual attention

- Responsiveness - people are willing to help and go the extra mile.

Collectively, these are known by the acronym, 'RATER'.

Note that all are people-orientated!

If customers want the organisations with which they deal to possess these faculties, who conceives and creates them within the organisation? It is, of course, the leaders and managers. However, all too often in our experience, such managers are far removed from the customer. Despite the popularity of TV programmes featuring managers working on the shop floor (literally in the case of some retailers featured), these instances are relatively infrequent. At the very least, they need to be engaging with those in their organisation who deal most frequently and intensively with the customer in order to stand any chance of building the characteristics listed above.

Acknowledging another seminal piece of research in the customer service environment, i.e. 'Putting the Service-Profit Chain to Work'[24], managers need to appreciate the concept of internal service within the *system* of their own organisation. Do HR, IT or Finance really appreciate how they affect the performance expectations of the end-user customer?

In Harper Lee's magnificent book, *To Kill a Mockingbird*, the lead character, Atticus Finch, remarks, "You never really understand a person until you consider things from his point of view... until you climb into his skin and walk around in it." Do people in organisations get into their customers' skins? Oddly, all are customers, very often of the organisation for which they work. Do they truly contemplate what is good, bad, indifferent and mediocre? Absolutely! A short conversation can throw out abundant examples of the good, the bad and the ugly.

Good show, bad show

One bank with which I worked adopted practice from the Walt Disney organisation in encouraging teams to conduct 'good show, bad show' discussions. These required team members to talk about their experiences, good and bad, when they were outside of work and being customers of other organisations. What did they experience that they liked (the 'good shows'), what did they encounter that they didn't like (the 'bad shows')? Out of these discussions, many new ideas to improve service quality were conceived and implemented. This practice was a key constituent in this business improving its profit three-fold over five years.

The community's expectations

Many organisations are the fulcrum of the communities in which they operate. They provide employment and generate the wealth that enables other businesses to function effectively, e.g. suppliers, shops and services. The community debate is both local and global and now tends to be captured under the label of Corporate Social Responsibility (CSR).

This is a highly contentious area into which we do not intend to wade too deeply because it is heavily weighted with political and emotional sentiment. That the strategist Michael Porter is now writing about the link between CSR and organisational performance cannot be dismissed[25]. CSR is becoming an increasingly important yardstick by which customers, staff (both prospective and existing) and investors choose the organisations they will deal with. Will the organisation that pollutes profligately or shifts all its production to lower cost locations and treats its staff shabbily sustain itself in the longer term? That question is asked somewhat rhetorically rather than as a means of providing a convenient springboard to take my narrative into this vipers' pit of debate.

However, from the perspective of performance evaluation, the topic cannot be overlooked and, indeed, forms the basis of a major study by the Centre for Tomorrow's Company (CfTC is a leading not-for-profit think-tank)[26] which is delving deeply into determining the challenges that organisations will face as the 21st century unfolds.

Conclusions

Having outlined various perspectives about performance, coupled with consideration of the core motives that drive both organisations and individuals to exercise effort in order to achieve their intended performance outcomes, I now intend to move on and start to consider comprehensively the answers to the following crucial questions:

- What needs to be put in place to achieve the defined performance goals, however they are derived?

- How are the performance goals achieved?

Before moving on to the next chapter, what do you think?

This chapter has considered performance from a number of angles including various profit and non-profit perspectives, together with various stakeholders and individuals involved in an organisation's life. However, performance is defined, our work shows two very clear facts:

1. In order for an organisation to achieve its outcomes, its leaders and managers need to create the right type of conditions in which people can perform effectively, flourish and prosper financially and/or developmentally.

2. Whether we are talking about an individual or a team context, there is no doubt that employees at all levels are highly motivated to perform and contribute to their organisation achieving its goals and fulfil its purpose.

In the next chapter, consideration is given to the idea of creating the optimal conditions in the context of what we will define as Climate and a 'Leadership Dynamic' that creates these conditions. In so doing, I shall distinguish between the more often considered concept of culture and climate and illustrate why it is important to maintain this distinction and why it is climate far more than culture that is the accelerator of performance.

CHAPTER 2:

People and the Climate in which they operate:
'The People Dimension'

From a research and consultancy perspective, my work started in the early 1980s in the manufacturing sector. At this time, the economics of the manufacturing environment were extremely challenging. It was clear that sustainable competitive advantage could be gained through the innovative exploitation (note, this is not using the word in its more pejorative tenor to infer mistreatment or abuse) of human capital as well as focusing on strategic planning, technology, brand management, and just-in-time production practices, etc. This is not an 'either/or' choice but one of sizeable increment.

I developed a practical approach for the management of the people side of the organisation, called the 'The People Dimension'. The key focus for organisational leaders concerns how they create an environment in their organisation in which innovation and creativity are fostered so that people feel a genuine sense of ownership and pride in what they do. They also recognise that their contribution helps their organisation out-perform its competitors.

As the eighties morphed into the nineties, other business sectors began to experience similar challenges to those just witnessed in manufacturing. How competitive advantage was gained and sustained no longer remained restricted to managing technology and brand. For example, in 1992 Barclays Bank plc (see that year's accounts) failed to make a profit for the first time and this represented a significant motivation for the bank to change how it managed its people. Indeed, financial services as a whole began to consider this process very actively, with the insurance sector particularly coming on board towards the end of decade.

The critical question revolves around demonstrating a clear alignment and correlation between investing in improving the entire process of managing an organisation's human capital and bottom line performance, be that in the commercial sector or the public sector. In either circumstance, it is essential that organisations optimise their financial efficiencies.

The idea of a performance *Climate*

As organisations and the individuals within them strive to achieve their desired performance objectives, their activities are affected by a range of business circumstances such as competitors, global economic cycles etc.

While such obvious factors are important, our work has shown that there is a critical leadership dynamic that drives a business almost irrespective of prevailing market conditions. Our research shows that all things being equal, the idea of 'Climate' in an organisation or workgroup is a significant driver of business performance.

By Climate we mean the nature of how people feel about working in a particular enterprise in terms of their focus, commitment and pride to be part of it. This sense of feeling is fundamentally affected by the nature of how individual managers or management teams behave. This is illustrated in Figure 2.1.

The Glowinkowski Integrated Framework

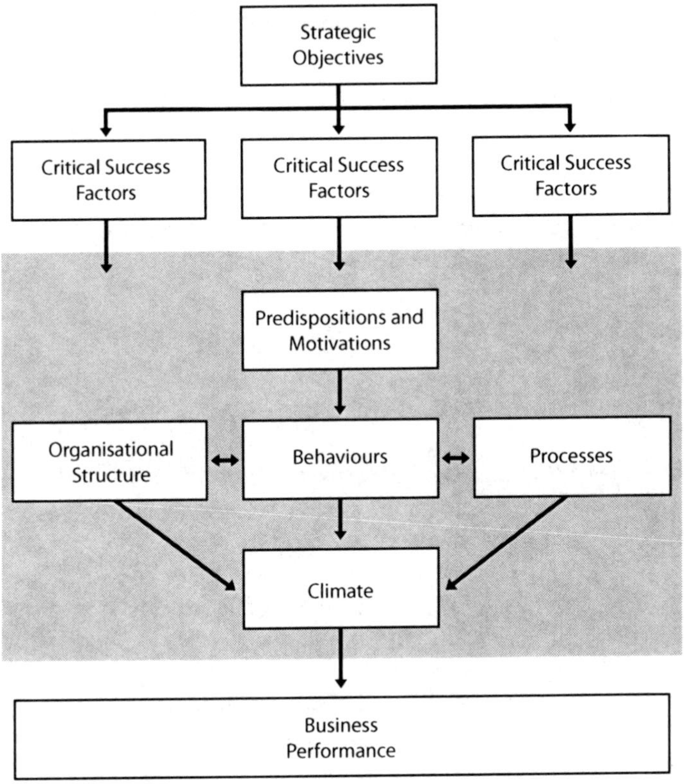

Figure 2.1

The Integrated Framework positions the idea of Climate as being the principal driver for the achievement of outstanding business performance.

In the context of this framework, Climate is defined as:

'What it feels like to work here'.

It is different from, but interdependent with the concept of Culture, which we recognise as relating to:

'How things are done here'.

Definition and measurement

In talking about the idea of Climate it is critical to have a clear and consistent understanding of the concept in order to facilitate measurement. As stated in the Introduction, the old adage that "unless you can measure something, you can't change it" is entirely apposite.

A quantitative questionnaire is used to measure an organisation's Climate, from which a small sample of questions is shown in Figure 2.2.

People feel:

- That there is a clear long-term direction for the business

- That they are encouraged to try out new ways of solving problems

- They can take action before being directed

- They are able to take decisions without always having to check with their boss

- There is a sense of a link between reward and effort

- That long- and short-term goals are communicated and discussed

- The long-term business direction is well understood

- They are confident in taking calculated risks

- They are ready to change the way they do things

- They are responsible for the accuracy of their work.

Figure 2.2

In the context of the Integrated Framework, Climate is represented by these types of feelings, which are a result of the overall *leadership dynamic*. From our measurement work with clients, two very clear connections are made:

1. All things being equal, Climate differentiates an average from an outstandingly performing organisation, i.e. two apparently similar organisations by, say, size and activity, may be delivering markedly different levels of performance where the higher performing organisation is underpinned by a measurably higher level of Climate.

2. Whatever the level of performance currently being achieved by an organisation, an improvement in its Climate will improve its performance measured across a range of bottom-line outcomes such as sales, customer service, productivity/efficiency etc. To be more specific, a measurable, positive shift in leadership behaviours will drive a quantifiable improvement in the Climate. In a commercial enterprise, an inviolate result of this Climate improvement is that the bottom-line numbers get better (and, from our consultancy experience, this occurs in times of economic growth and contraction).

A sense of what's possible

In one case study within a Call Centre environment, a measurable and positive shift in leadership behaviours caused a measureable uplift in the Climate. In turn, this caused an improvement in the behaviours of the staff talking to the customers on the telephone. Over a relatively short period of time, a doubling of the call/sales ratio was witnessed. Whereas before it took 24 calls to generate a sale, after our intervention only 12 calls were required to achieve a sale. This was in a heavily-regulated environment, so it was not possible to impose a 'hard sell'. Enhanced service performance arising from better behaviours drove the sales growth. Through external assessment, customer service quality improved, moving from 55% of customers being very satisfied to 89% being very satisfied.

This enhanced behaviour and Climate was sustained over several years until the business was sold.

A model of Climate

Climate was initially coined as a concept in the late 1950s and 1960s. More recent comments have been made by the likes of Burke and Litwin[27], and Ekvall[28]. In a more generalist style, Daniel Goleman[29] makes reference, too.

The Integrated Framework has been conceived from research and consultancy work during a quarter of a century working in partnership with a wide range of international and global organisations. The key focus was always to establish a framework that is grounded in the common sense reality of practical organisational life, which can be used to help managers to improve performance. In turn, this provides an accurate and valid source of benchmark measurement; managers can know how well they are doing compared to other organisations.

Climate represents 'what it feels like to work in a particular team or organisation'. It represents the *mood* or *atmosphere* that prevails within a given work environment. Climate manifests the output that occurs from three critical inputs or 'change levers', which include:

- the behaviour of the manager/management team

- the effectiveness of the organisation's structure and job design

- the effectiveness of the processes.

Improved performance is the outcome of enhanced Climate.

Let us get one thing straight: I am not suggesting that Climate equates to some ethereal, nebulous 'happy, clappy' mood. In words of very few syllables, an effective Climate is 'the key state that lets an organisation perform well'.

Our experience demonstrates:

- *Strong Climate equates to high performance,* whereas

- *Weak Climate equates to low performance*

Climate comprises six core dimensions, which are summarised in Table 2.1.

I am now going to spend some time discussing these different elements of Climate. I encourage you to work through the following pages and to consider how strong each dimension of Climate is in your own organisation. This should provide a rich learning experience for you and help you build a deep understanding of this material.

Table 2.1: A DEFINITION OF THE FACTORS OF CLIMATE

FACTORS	MEANING
CLARITY	People *feel* a sense of clear understanding about what their organisation is trying to achieve and how they contribute to this purpose and the associated goals and objectives.
CHALLENGE	People *feel* a sense of working towards challenging yet realistic goals. There is a view that they are appropriately 'stretched' in terms of the contribution they are expected to make.
CHANGE ORIENTATION	People *regard* change in a positive manner and that, as a result, they can invoke action and change how things are done with ease.
AUTONOMY	People *feel* a sense of ownership and responsibility for the outcomes of their work and that they do not always have to get the permission of their boss before they make a decision or take action.
RECOGNITION	People *experience* a link between effort, outcome and reward and, through effective feedback, feel that they are valued and appreciated. They feel empowered to do a good job.
INVOLVEMENT	People *experience* a sense of real commitment to their organisation's purpose and objectives; they feel proud to be working for the organisation.

Clarity

The Clarity that exists within any organisation or component business unit, function or team provides a sense of purpose and direction for the people working there. Essentially, people acquire a clear appreciation for how their own work relates to that of their colleagues and the overall aims of the organisation. They gain a deep understanding between 'what I do' and what the organisation is striving to achieve. In other words, it provides them with due reason and explanation for why they are being asked to do what they are doing.

The most famous allegory concerning an organisation possessing Clarity involves US President J.F. Kennedy visiting NASA in Florida after making his famous speech incepting the Apollo missions to the moon*. During the visit, he encountered a man sweeping the floor and the conversation is alleged to have gone something like, "What are you doing?" "I'm helping send a man to the moon, Mr President." "But you're sweeping the floor, sir." "Yes, I know, Mr President, but I have to keep this place spotless so the rocket isn't contaminated with dirt."

Keeping it clean:

Slightly more down to earth (sic), a colleague describes a cleaner in Liverpool who was in her fifties and had had a hip replacement operation. She asked her manager if she could return to work because she thought it the best means of convalescing from her operation. In terms of Clarity, however, her decision was influenced by her understanding of the business' determination to deliver superb service to its customers. In her mind, delivering good service to external customers meant that the quality of service within the business had to be top-notch, too. She considered this included keeping the toilets and washrooms spic-and-span, which was a key part of her cleaning responsibility. She considered herself to be 'the best loo cleaner in the business' so she had to get back to work to prevent standards falling and staff becoming unhappy. In her mind, if this happened external customers would be served less well because staff would think the organisation didn't care about them and the facilities in which they worked.

To build Clarity means succeeding in helping everyone in the organisation to

---

* In an address to Congress on May 25, 1961, President Kennedy said, "I believe that this nation should commit itself to achieving the goal, before this decade is out, of landing a man on the Moon and returning him safely to the Earth. No single space project in this period will be more impressive to mankind, or more important for the long-range exploration of space; and none will be so difficult or expensive to accomplish."

possess a crystal clear understanding about why the organisation exists and what it is trying to achieve. This can be couched as purpose, vision or mission statements supported by goals, aims and objectives.

Whatever lexicon is used, Clarity measures the extent to which such statements of intent are understood. Most critically, however, Clarity embraces the degree to which individuals relate to how their own role contributes to the fulfilment of such organisational aims.

Through Clarity, people in the organisation gain a sense of its 'long-term direction' and see that everyone's activities are both 'integrated' and 'co-ordinated' towards achieving the over-arching goals. In a recovery or turn-round situation, it may well be that the 'long-term direction' is relatively short-term in that some immediate actions have to be taken to stabilise the enterprise. It is only when this is starting to be achieved that a longer-term perspective can begin to be set. Where strong Clarity exists, people are far better placed to make decisions because they are keenly aware about what they need to do in order to make the fullest possible contribution to their organisation being successful.

True north

Horst Schultze, former CEO of Ritz-Carlton Hotels, talked of people and activities as being 'pointed true north' (told to a colleague during a customer service benchmarking visit to a Ritz-Carlton hotel). A simple metaphorical exercise he conducted spells this out. Get, say, 20 people to stand up, ask them to close their eyes and turn three times to the left, then three times to the right, then ask them to point to the north. The likely outcome is that each will point in a different direction.

In organisational Climate terms, this analogously represents lousy Co-ordination.

The performance implications of Clarity

- When people experience a strong level of Clarity within their organisation it provides a powerful foundation for high performance and the opportunity for people to deliver to their fullest potential.

- Without Clarity in place, people are unclear about what they need to concentrate upon. They do not appreciate the priorities.

- People may feel that they are working in a vacuum and so possess a real sense of 'what's the point, it doesn't really matter'. By their own volition, because they do not know otherwise, they could head off down an entirely inappropriate route.

- We often observe sales teams operating with low Clarity focusing their actions on selling the products that are easier to sell rather than the ones that are more profitable.

- The overall performance outcome for an organisation with low Clarity is lack of competitive edge and prioritisation about use of resource.

The Clarity dimension represents the single most important element of the Climate model. Without Clarity, there is little that one can expect in terms of building up the strength of the other five dimensions.

Challenge

The second factor in the framework of Climate is Challenge. This relates to the extent to which people feel energised and challenged within their organisation or team. A high score indicates that people believe that doing excellent, quality work is encouraged, and that delivering outstanding performance is genuinely valued.

Organisations scoring highly in this area of Climate will demonstrate significant 'innovation' through its people trying new ways of solving problems and overcoming challenges. People are prepared to challenge the status quo in terms of how things are done, without fearing they will be criticised for 'rocking the boat'. As new things are tried but which don't work out, lessons are learnt rather than people blamed. Such an ethos of challenge perhaps flies in the face of 'Quality' (note our deliberate use of the capital Q) because its underlying mantra of 'do it right, first time, every time' can, in our experience, staunch innovation. Yes, things have to be done right, but there is always likely to be some further improvement opportunity.

Research from the world of education[*] [and 30] has for many years shown that memory and physical (or doing) learning is often more effective when you get it right first time, i.e. it is often difficult to learn a new golf swing or learn a new telephone

[*] Sylvia Downs conceived the 'MUD' acronym representing different approaches to learning, where M = memory learning, i.e. better to get right first time, U = understanding learning, which is better to get wrong and realise it, and D = doing learning which, like memory, is better to get right first time – think about trying to correct a golf swing!

number. However, conceptual (or understanding) learning has been shown to be more successful when the individual gets it wrong first time. This reinforces the need to destroy the blame culture that prevails in so many organisations. People need to be able to make mistakes in order to learn.

If at first you don't succeed:

A nice piece of understanding learning is seen in some of the 'champion/ challenger' techniques applied to debt collection, where samples of customers are selected for different styles of approach to be made. By limiting the size of these samples, mistakes can be made without incurring significant losses. Those approaches which do work can then be more confidently applied to a wider cross- section of customers.

People will also feel that they are stimulated by their work and, accordingly, are prepared to work hard in order to 'achieve' fantastic results. They are 'up for the challenge' and will want to put in extra effort in order to achieve their stretching goals and objectives, which they have agreed with their manager as opposed to their being imposed.

The human need for challenge

It has long been recognised that human beings need to have personal objectives and purpose, i.e. a sense of 'what's the point?' or a 'raison d'être'. It is a natural human condition for individuals to strive for objectives that are challenging but at the same time realistic. Research in objective setting shows a natural tendency for individuals of all ages to set goals for themselves that have an 80% chance of success and a 20% chance of failure. This, indeed, is the healthy option.

It is perhaps not surprising to see the many anecdotal illustrations of children of very successful and wealthy parents who find life difficult; living up to the expectations of their mother or father is damned near impossible yet their wealth provides no reason to.

We have encountered many thousands of individuals in organisations and it is clear that folk enjoy being appropriately energised. This is the focus of the Challenge dimension of Climate. Indeed, it sounds trite but the vast majority of people like to feel they are doing a good job.

This desire for a challenge, which has a good chance of success, neatly tallies with the 'R' in the acronym 'SMART'*, which is often referred to in the field of goal and target setting.

- **S** relates to the goal being Specific

- **M** relates to the goal being Measurable

- **A** relates to the goal being Attainable

- **R** relates to the goal being Realistic, i.e. 80% chance of success and 20% chance of failure.

- **T** relates to the goal being Timely, i.e. it has to be achieved by a certain point rather than 'whenever'.

The performance implications of Challenge

- When people experience a strong level of Challenge, they have the opportunity to use their skills fully, particularly in the context of trying new, innovative and creative approaches to resolving problems.

- Innovation is stimulated and encouraged by staff being given space and time to think of new ideas and approaches. As a result, new product development can be done more quickly; the causes of mistakes are identified, understood and eliminated rapidly.

- When an organisation is characterised by a poor level of Challenge, individuals find themselves massively under-utilised. Consequently, they are liable to become bored and frustrated in their roles and are more likely to make mistakes, which could have catastrophic consequences.

- Additionally, low 'scoring' organisations do not get their 'full money's worth of contribution' from their human capital by virtue of it not being optimally employed. As a direct result, overall economic performance is not as good as it could be.

* The derivation of this well known acronym does not appear to be specifically attributed.

- Furthermore, we observe talent 'making for the door' in pursuit of career opportunities that will make best use of their hard-won qualifications and skills. This drives up staff turnover, producing a further economic drain and likely diminution in customer service quality because replacement staff have to be trained.

The key point to make about a Climate of low Challenge is that the behavioural capabilities of the employees are never fully realised, so that part of the fundamental human condition of wanting to be part of something successful is never going to be attained.

Change orientation

It would be easy to interpret the preceding two dimensions of Climate as inferring that organisations need to be absolutely steadfast in driving towards set aims. This is so to a degree but, given the pace at which markets now move (and this applies to the public sector where the array of performance targets shifts frequently due to political manipulation), it is equally important that organisations are adaptable and flexible in their approach.

This momentum is neatly encapsulated in remarks the author has heard attending numerous conference and symposiums. For instance, "Mankind has accumulated more knowledge since 1960 than in all preceding time"; "The half-life of today's knowledge is four years" (remarks heard by a colleague at a Tom Peters conference in the 1990s). Perhaps, that half-life has shrunk still further, which is a daunting thought! The greatest impetus has arisen from the domain of technology; for instance, on a tour of NASA's Cape Canaveral facility, a colleague recalls the tour guide saying, "The 'fuzzy logic' of a top-range washing machine relies on more computer processing power than Neil Armstrong had in the capsule of Apollo 11." That more computing power is now applied to the washing of laundry than to conveying three men 500,000 miles across the void of space is a massively palpable demonstration of technological advancement and its effect upon the dynamics of every business and market sector.

For organisations, standing still is not a viable option; Darwin's theory of survival applies![31]

The concept of Change Orientation as part of the Climate framework is, therefore, clearly very critical. First and foremost, people in the organisation need to be willing or 'motivated' to take action and change how things are done. They possess initiative and when this prevails at the ground-floor level of an organisation, 'magic' can occur because the organisation becomes a hive of activity in terms of delivering 'business as usual' as well as initiating change. Employees are truly interested and compelled to improve the work that they do.

Ball bearings should be perfectly round!

Some years ago, one manager we worked with in a retail environment recalls visiting a factory that made ball bearings. Far too many bearings were rejected at the end of the production process. The machine operatives had suggested to managers that a check could be made during the process, which would help reduce the rate of failure. Their suggestions were rejected. However, motivated to improve their factory's performance, the engineers took it upon themselves to establish their own checking facility alongside the production line, using old benches and some rudimentary callipers. After a few days, managers noticed that rejection rates were falling markedly and went to the factory shop-floor to try to ascertain what was happening. They quickly found out.

While this anecdote conveys a number of idioms, the one being stressed is the motivation of the machine operatives to improve performance.

High scoring Change Orientation organisations succeed in keeping unnecessary systems and procedures to a minimum; they are 'adaptable' and 'flexible'. Decisions to change are not delayed. Procedures are used as guidelines for action rather than tight control. This does not mean taking things into one's own hands and potentially breaking laws and compliance rules. Instead, the people across the organisation manifestly emit a willingness and enthusiasm not to allow the grass to grow under their feet. They are keen to have the opportunity to be involved in new activities, and do not suffocate new ideas at birth by imposing stifling bureaucracy and draconian rules.

Never satisfied

One manager we worked with at a major UK bank, who had previously worked in an FMCG environment for the organisation holding second largest market share regarded with envy the Change Orientation of the market leader. She remarked, "They're number one, but they always think like the number two wanting to catch up and overtake themselves. Their energy is staggering. The initiative that their most junior employees apply is impressive."

The performance implication of Change Orientation

- When people experience a strong level of Change Orientation there is a clear sense of people being able to make improvements. Often this results in the organisation demonstrating a powerful adaptability and deft touch in its customer engagement.

- Because change is regarded as exciting and motivating by the significant majority of people, they are keen to consider new ways of doing things; they want the organisational *culture* to change. (Remember, we distinguish culture as being 'how things are done', i.e. it relates to the organisation's systems, procedures, protocols, and practices.)

Why do so many culture change programmes fail?

Because the people dimension and, specifically, this factor of Climate has, at best, been overlooked; at worst, completely ignored. There are a few fundamentals that need to be remembered with any change programme; they are that people don't change unless:

- They see the point

- They see the benefit for themselves and the organisation

- The benefits of the change exceed the pain of effecting the change[* and 32].

These conditions underpin individuals' enthusiasm and willingness to change.

By the way, if as a leader you do not recognise this, then resign and do everyone a favour!

- Organisational resource is continually available to help facilitate change. This is not to suggest that there are people on stand-by doing nothing until a change request is initiated but, rather, that the organisation is able to assemble new teams or re-allocate resources to different activities with relative ease. Consequently, organisations possess dexterity and momentum to respond quickly to emerging market forces. In the very high scoring organisations, this faculty enables them to pre-empt emerging customer requirements and steal a march on the competition.

- In a Climate marked by low Change Orientation, individuals feel frustrated that any new ideas they generate are likely to get stuck in the 'organisational treacle'. Much vaunted ideas and schemes grind to a halt because employees consider them to be brakes rather than accelerators of change. The organisation can miss the boat in the face of a fast-changing business environment.

---

* See The Change Model or Change Formula by Richard Beckhard, Reuben T. Harris, attributed to David Gleicher. D x V x F > R where D = dissatisfaction with current situation, V = vision of an alternative, F = first steps and R = resistance to change. Until the resistance to change is exceeded by the perceived benefits, resistance will win through.

Finally, having high Change Orientation does not mean being an organisation that flits *will-o'-the-wisp*-like between incepting initiatives and not delivering anything. Change needs to be purposeful and objective and, in the main, carried through to implementation. However, having high Change Orientation may enable organisations to recognise when 'enough is enough' and certain change activities have to be canned because they are progressing too slowly. Where this condition does not prevail, large unwieldy and lumbering change initiatives are allowed to continue despite the fact they will never deliver the initially anticipated benefits. Scarce resource remains locked in place rather than being released to more vital and viable activities. This stasis seems especially prevalent in the public sector.

Autonomy

This dimension of Climate relates to the idea of the difference that people feel they can make to the performance of the organisation or team of which they are a member. People who feel a sense of Autonomy feel capable and empowered to do things for themselves; taking responsibility for the outcomes of their work and not having to always check with another before taking action or making decisions. There is an absence of 'learned helplessness'[33].

Learned helplessness

The term was coined in the field of psychiatry following the treatment of holocaust victims during the Second World War. Essentially, the complete lack of freedom to act over a long period of time (this is, admittedly, a minimalist definition) causes people to give up the option of flight and enter a depressed state of resignation, which ultimately becomes a state of 'learned helplessness'. This psychological process has been well-documented in various fields and while its origin is somewhat exceptional, nevertheless we see less dramatic examples in the workplace. Individuals with little or no opportunity for empowerment simply resign themselves to turning the handle of mediocrity with a sense of little opportunity to make a difference.

A simple indicator of organisational Autonomy is provided when we all remove our organisational caps and replace them with that of being a customer. What experience do you encounter when you have a problem? Is it resolved readily and easily by the first person you encounter or is achieving resolution as difficult as pushing water up a hill? The former suggests organisational Autonomy, the latter suggests otherwise!

For Autonomy to exist, first of all individuals need to feel able to make decisions themselves and not refer everything 'up-the-line' to their boss. This sense of *'independence'* provides people with the confidence and appropriate authority to take responsibility for their work. This is important in the context of matrix structures where it can be all too easy to lose sight of such responsibilities. This is not to say everyone does their own thing. The independence concerns fulfilling one's responsibility to achieving the goals of the organisation. Where there is Autonomy and <u>no</u> Clarity, there can be anarchy. Where both prevail, people will feel comfortable and confident in accepting *'accountability'*. People will happily assume responsibility for the outcomes of their work; they will be the first to admit if they have fallen short of what is expected.

Where a strong level of Autonomy exists, a greater frequency of people doing more than expected is observed. They put in immense *'effort'* to do more than is expected. We are essentially making a distinction between what tends to be called the *expected* and the *discretionary* contribution.

The computer says "no"

Stealing a famous punch-line from the UK comedy series, 'Little Britain', highlights an incident in a contact centre we worked with in the late 1990s where the systems appeared to be declining profitable business. A group of staff took it upon themselves to look into matters more thoroughly and found a glitch in the system. They did this working through lunch breaks and into evenings without claiming overtime. Their solution was worth tens of millions of pounds. This combined Independence and Accountability was acknowledged and rewarded.

The performance implications of Autonomy

- A high score in Autonomy indicates that people feel they can individually make a real difference to the performance of their team or organisation. The prevailing mindset is a 'can do/will do' attitude as opposed to resignation or, indeed, the idea of learned helplessness.

- When people experience a strong level of Autonomy in their organisation, they feel they can make decisions without threat of censure for doing so. The pace at which decisions are made across the organisations is fast.

- People possess a sense of personal responsibility for the outcomes of their work, including the decisions they have made. They will hold up their hands and not try to lay off the blame on to colleagues (or customers) for anything that has gone wrong.

- People feel more than willing (note, _not_ coerced) to work above and beyond the defined remit of their job, which is, of course, the _expected_ contribution, and are prepared 'to go the extra mile' and make discretionary delivery.

- Organisations with low Autonomy create a type of learned helplessness where individuals need to check before they do anything and feel compelled to follow the rules to the letter. We have heard many times in Focus Groups the sentiment expressed by employees that they feel they are obliged to leave their brains in the cloakroom before coming on to the factory shop-floor.

- High Autonomy correlates with strong safety records in manufacturing and construction, innovation in school class-rooms and, as the following neat little case study demonstrates, excellent customer service. (In organisations scoring very highly in Autonomy, this service ethic extends throughout the organisation; because people appreciate how they serve each other, this affects the ultimate service received by the external client.)

Route 66, or at least the A66

An Advisor in a bank's contact centre personally delivered documentation to a customer on her way home and collected it the following morning on her way into work. Why? So that the customer could complete the purchase of his dream car, a mint-condition 1950's Cadillac. (It turned out that both the Advisor and the customer were fans of Elvis and she understood why the customer so wanted the car!)

Simply, this entire dimension is all about people delivering the discretionary as well as the expected contribution.

Recognition

Recognition is the fifth factor in the Climate framework. It represents the idea of whether the organisation is a true meritocracy. When people feel they work within a climate of recognition they have a clear sense of a differential relationship between performance and reward. Effort is appropriately rewarded and malingering is addressed and tackled. In this type of environment, effective performance is achieved because there is a strong, effective and constructive feedback process. As a result, individuals understand how they are doing. People feel that their efforts are valued and appreciated.

For a high score to emerge in this factor, people need to believe that there is a real, genuine and tangible link between what they contribute in terms of effort and result, and the *'reward'* they receive. Reward, development and promotion are all dependent on how well they do in their job. In this type of differential environment, people realise that extra effort will be recognised and, as a result, it is worth putting in the effort. In this context, the reward is likely to be financial but we find that it is not the absolute level of reward but rather its differential relationship with performance. An alternative reward we see frequently is organisations sponsoring development education. The key point for people, however, is that the effort they put in is reflected in what they get back.

In my experience, more often than not, people want to know how they are doing. Receiving timely, relevant, objective, constructive *'feedback'* is a vital ingredient in people feeling their organisation is a meritocracy. However, all too often we find organisations' feedback processes to be ineffectual because they are carried out half-heartedly. Managers simply go through the motions; they do not engage with appropriate impact or conviction because they regard giving feedback as a necessary evil. Their lacklustre approach adds no value to the recipient; if anything it is more harmful. In this type of environment, feedback may exist but there is no differential relationship relating to performance contribution.

Organisations that have created strong and effective feedback processes tend to be populated with individuals who welcome the opportunity to discuss meaningfully how to improve their performance through accentuating their strengths and addressing their weaknesses. In having such opportunities, people are able to look forward and acquire a sense of how they are regarded and thought of in terms of current performance and future potential.

In organisations scoring highly in this Climate factor, there is a palpable sense of people feeling they are *'valued and appreciated'*. The phrase 'our people are our greatest asset' has substance for them, rather than it being shallow rhetoric.

Gotcha!

One client took an idea from a US hospital they visited. Called the 'Gotcha-gram', it was a simple fold-over card in which a personal note of thanks could be conveyed by one team member to another - be that boss to team member, peer to peer - to express appreciation, gratitude or praise (and sometimes to apologise for a mistake made). This was hand-written and left on desks or dispatched via the internal mail. E-mail didn't detract from its use because it was considered much more personal.

The performance implications of Recognition

- When people experience strong Recognition in terms of Climate, they sense there is a clear link between high effort and high reward and that poor performance is tackled.

- There will be no sense of nepotism or favouritism being the cause of promotion; instead it is won on merit. The age-old debilitating habit of people being promoted because it 'shifts a problem' is diffused. Neither is promotion achieved simply by length of tenure, i.e. the 'it's her turn now' syndrome is removed.

- Where there is weak Recognition, organisations develop a malaise with the result that excellence, e.g. in service quality, fades away.

- Staff turnover increases in organisations having low Recognition scores; indeed it is one of the primary causal factors of high turnover. As a result, the organisation is unlikely to be viewed as an 'employer of choice' and it becomes more difficult to recruit the requisite talent.

Halving staff turnover

A financial services organisation had in excess of 60% staff turnover in its Contact Centre. Upon seeing that Recognition was poorly regarded by their people (it was in the bottom quartile of our international database when we measured it) the leadership team was galvanised to take action. We tracked the progress of this intervention over the next six months and were able to show that a clear upward trend in this particular Climate score was married to a marked downward trend in staff turnover.

Fascinatingly, this situation had not been spotted in the organisation's own Staff Survey conducted in each of the preceding three years, which says much about the poverty of information provided by most staff surveys![*]

Involvement

The final member of this 'big six' set of Climate factors is the Idea of Involvement. This relates to the extent to which people feel a sense of buy-in and *'commitment'* to the aims, objectives and long-term direction of the organisation. Team members implicitly and explicitly *'trust'* and so they know they can depend on each other to work collaboratively and in a manner that no one wants to let down anyone else. People have pride and enjoy being part of the organisation, together with a sense of real collectivism in terms of there being a true team. People believe that the combination of talents in the team works as a complete entity, which is immensely greater than the sum of the parts, i.e. there is *'synergy'*.

[*] Measuring Climate is a much more effective means of gathering the view of staff across an organisation. The responses are all related to the six dimensions of Climate that have a direct bearing upon organisational performance. The data is actionable and improvements in Climate feed directly through to performance. This is not the case with the majority of staff surveys we have seen, which appear to be little more than a sop to canvassing staff opinion. If members of staff are asked their views, they do not want to be patronised by not seeing any response taken. Our measure of Climate does not run such a risk.

Ashes to ashes

In 2005, the English cricket team beat the Australians in the five-day Test series and took back the Ashes after many years' absence from these shores. Even the most disinterested cricket observer will have been aware of this series and how the English cricket team was truly characterised by a high level of Involvement. They behaved in a way that demonstrated a commitment and motivation to the purpose, i.e. winning back the Ashes, and achieving a first step in retaining them, together with a real sense of *teamness* where individuals played to their strengths, where the sum of cricketing parts was truly greater as a whole. They were, incidentally, also inspired by an excellent leadership team in the form of team captain and coach. In short, they experienced the Climate dimension of Involvement which resulted in the achievement of winning the Ashes against the opposition of what many considered a superior Australian team.

Eighteen months later, in the heat of the Australian sun, that powerful leadership dynamic had clearly dipped (some would say predictably, but that is too sensitive, sorry Lancashire fans!) The result was a collapse in the Climate of Involvement and certainly a lack of a clear sense of team members buying into a common vision such as prevailed in 2005.

The performance implications of Involvement

- When people experience a strong level of Involvement, the degree of passion for the organisation is palpable. People feel personally slighted if there is bad press. The drive to resolve complaints and avoid losing a valuable customer is very strong. Where complaints arise, people work together collectively to sort out the matter, to understand why the problem arose and to introduce measures to prevent recurrence.

- A high score also indicates that teams across the organisation believe they contribute value; they consider they are doing something worthwhile that will demonstrably feed into the organisation achieving its aims.

- A low score suggests that individuals think they have been grouped together for some obscure organisational convenience. Equally, a low score may represent that the team considers it has come to the end of its useful life and should be adjourned or stood down. This is especially severe if coupled with low Change Orientation. We observe too many organisations keeping teams together for too long and members becoming disillusioned in having no real purpose.

- A low score in Involvement is clearly correlated with an organisation possessing a 'silo mentality'. People guard their patch and are reluctant to support each other and share knowledge. Internal service can be poor, not just between a function and the main business area but also between different sections of the main production process. Quite often one area can be trying to improve a particular practice that has already been tried elsewhere. In really severe cases, we see an ironic glee emerge in the area that first tried to make the improvement and failed, see another fall at the same hurdle. Organisational learning[34] is conspicuous by its absence.

- Low Involvement can be catastrophic. People are apathetic, complacent and, potentially, disruptive. Within and across teams, there is a sense of dysfunctionality. Such lack of involvement can all too easily spill over into the customer base by virtue of their feeling the organisation's staff don't especially care about them.

- People regard the senior management population to have lost the plot about what the overall aims and objectives need to be. In terms of the earlier example about Ritz-Carlton, people are pointing to all points of the compass rather than 'true north'!

Summary of the Climate framework and performance consequences

Clarity	Lack of priority
Challenge	Poor innovation
Change Orientation	Poor responsiveness to change
Autonomy	Inefficiencies and mistakes abound
Recognition	Talent walks; recruitment is difficult
Involvement	Poor internal support and service

Figure 2.3

Figure 2.3 shows a simple summary of the Climate framework, which I have just described. There are five conclusions to re-emphasise:

1. Climate dimensions represent what it feels like to work in an organisation.

2. Each Climate dimension drives bottom line performance outcomes.

3. If you can show measurable improvement in any Climate dimension you will get measurable improvement in bottom line performance.

4. The role of a manager in delivering leadership is ultimately to create a good Climate; in other words, a performance-orientated Climate.

5. The management of Climate is, therefore, our *leadership dynamic.*

In the next chapter, I will consider our *leadership dynamic* in detail.

CHAPTER 3:

The Leadership Dynamic

The previous chapter provided an account of the Climate framework. The key point is that Climate represents what it is like to be in an organisation and, from a measurement and definitional point of view, we have shown a clear correlation between each of these Climate dimensions and a raft of bottom line outcomes. The critical issue that I now wish to explore is the question of what creates and drives the Climate dimensions themselves.

Figure 3.1 shows again the Integrated Framework.

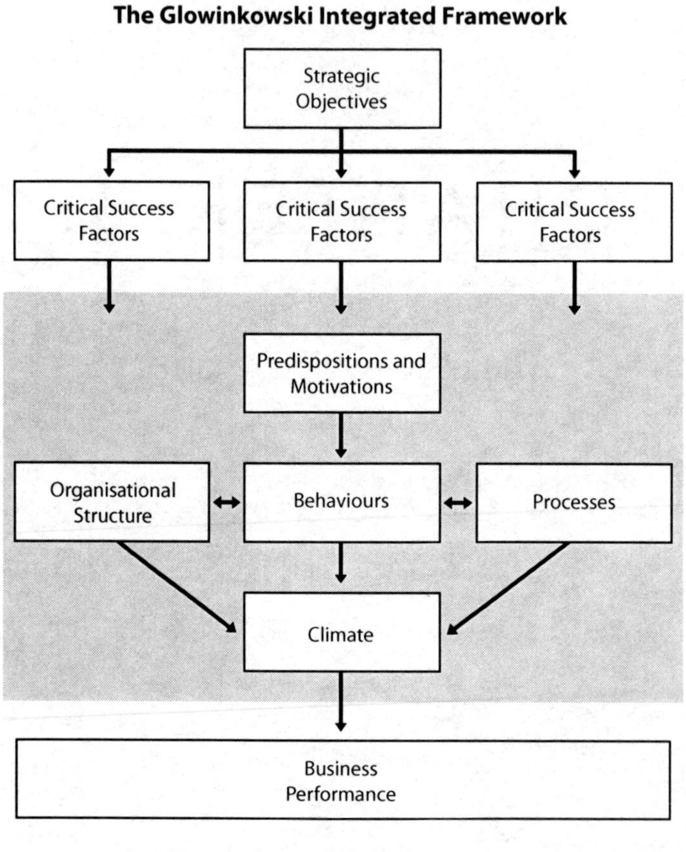

The Glowinkowski Integrated Framework

Figure 3.1

The model depicts Climate as being driven by three factors. These factors are:

1. Organisational structure

2. Behaviours (of managers and management teams)

3. Processes

I have mentioned already a number of times the diagnostic measurement and consultancy work that my colleagues and I have conducted with many organisations over the last 25 years. It is through these engagements that we have experienced the consistent relationship between the three factors of Organisation, Behaviour and Process in the creation of Climate. These three factors can be described as 'change levers'; they represent what happens within an organisation and thus drive Climate. Whether Climate is 'good' and the resultant organisational performance is strong is determined by how well each change lever is managed. Without wanting to be repetitive, let me repeat the critical points (!):

• Good Organisation creates good Climate creates good bottom line

• Good Behaviour by leaders and managers creates good Climate creates good bottom line

• Good Process creates good Climate creates good bottom line.

The idea of a *leadership dynamic* relates to exactly how these three change levers influence the Climate. Let me now explore this relationship in more detail.

Left hand/right hand

As an example of how Process and Behaviour should work hand-in-hand, leaders in one organisation were behaviourally addressing performance and identifying development needs. However, the organisation's process of documenting these needs and fulfilling them moved at the pace of treacle on a cold day. As a result, the employees considered Recognition was poor because development was not being provided.

Let me consider at further length each change lever in turn.

Organisational Structure/Job Design and its link to Climate

Design is becoming regarded as important in many areas of business and private life. How well designed are objects - e.g. cars, telephones, food containers, buildings - in terms of usability, aesthetics, efficiency and effectiveness? How does design contribute to the sustained success organisations have in their markets? The same rationale applies to how we design organisational structures and jobs. How well assembled is the organisation? How well defined are individual jobs in terms of their purpose and the skills, attributes and behaviours people need to be effective in them? How well do the jobs themselves challenge and motivate and so provide intrinsic job satisfaction to the jobholder? A favoured design in organisational structure these days is the matrix; does it work?

This element of the Integrated Framework focuses on all these aspects. These factors determine the nature of people's activities and represent behaviour from a structural perspective. The nature of these behaviours and practices will strongly impact both the Climate of the team and its performance.

The key issue is to recognise how these dimensions operate and the impact that they have. A summary of the framework of Organisational Structure and Job Design is presented in Table 3.1 while in Appendix 1 a more detailed specification is provided.

Table 3.1: A SUMMARY OF THE FACTORS OF ORGANISATIONAL STRUCTURE/JOB DESIGN

FACTORS	MEANING
STRUCTURE/ORGANISATION	The organisation is designed in such a way that the activities and responsibilities of individuals, teams, departments and functions do not overlap nor are they overlooked. The structure, while strong, possesses flexibility and an innate responsiveness to market dynamics, particularly involving customer needs and expectations. Spans of control are appropriate, ensuring sufficient distance between levels to help establish clear accountabilities. Standards of excellence are defined.
JOB CHARACTERISTICS	Jobs are not 'fractionalised' down to the lowest possible scale; in other words jobs are complete entities that possess significance when set against the organisation's intent. Jobs are defined in such a way that they permit the jobholder discretion and minimise the potential for conflict over confused accountabilities. Jobs make use of people's skills and abilities and, within themselves, provide feedback in terms of indicating whether the job has been done well.
MOTIVATION AND FEELINGS	Jobs provide the appropriate degree of challenge and volume of work. They provide fulfilment.

Within these three principal factors there is a range of specific measures that assess the effectiveness of Organisational Structure. The statistical correlation of each measure and each of the six factors of Climate has been established. This statistical relationship provides the foundation of what we call the 'Climate Dimension Matrix'.* A summary of this statistical analysis is provided in Appendix 2.

From the perspective of managing this component of the leadership dynamic, the point is quite simple: it is that each measure of Organisational Structure will have an impact on each factor of Climate. If an organisation's leadership is committed to improving performance, by measuring the efficacy of its structural design it can direct its focus to those areas scoring lowest and make improvements. These will have a direct impact upon Climate and, as I concluded the last chapter by saying, an increase in Climate causes performance to improve.

To bring this to life, let us consider some key relationships between this 'change lever' of our Leadership Dynamic and Climate.

Organisational Overlap

- This results when duplication of responsibility occurs. In an industrial paints organisation, I observed in one location that customer service was the responsibility, i.e. as defined in a job description, of the Marketing and the Finance functions. There was overlap and, indeed, each function recognised this as an issue and it was duly reflected as a negative score in the quantitative survey.

  As a result of this overlap, there was a very low score in terms of Autonomy because people did not feel they had the wherewithal to decide and implement action without checking. The fact was it was a very real problem. The dysfunctional organisational structure reduced people's feelings of Autonomy (in Climate) which, in this instance, created an issue in terms of poor customer service.

Organisational gaps

- This occurs when it is difficult to ascribe responsibility for a particular activity to a given individual or function. With a services business client, responsibility for certain aspects of customer service appeared to lurch between Sales and Customer Relations. Where an existing customer

* The Climate Dimension Matrix: Our statistical analysis of many years and many thousands of statistical collections shows that the significant majority all of these change lever factors demonstrate a positive correlation with the Climate dimensions. See Appendix 2 for a summary of the primary correlations.

called back to 'buy more', Sales wanted to provide the 'service'. However, where the customer was coming back with a problem, Sales wanted Customer Relations to handle the situation. Everyone in the business was cognisant of this position but was reluctant to do anything about it.

The problem was only properly surfaced and tackled as a result of measurement that we undertook. This elicited a poor sense of Clarity, i.e. who was there to provide a good service experience to the customer, which was clearly stated as a strategic intent of the business. Involvement was also weak because in designing the service delivery process, neither Sales nor Customer Relations had been appropriately consulted by the externally managed project team (which is another entirely different structural issue we often encounter that has serious implications for the strength of an organisation's Climate).

Headroom

- Another problem relates to poor quality headroom, which can be either due to there being too little headroom or too much between roles in an organisation. Too little headroom, i.e. a sense of being cramped is often seen in nascent matrix structures until they shake themselves out. Too much headroom is seen in situations where organisations have 'de-layered' and stretched spans of control to an excessive extent.

- In one client organisation, there was limited headroom between roles due to a poorly-designed matrix structure. Individual senior managers were 'cramped' in their style of decision making. As a result, the organisation's score for Change Orientation was very low.

  In practical terms, this meant people perceived the organisation was strangled by its own bureaucracy, which inhibited quick decision-making. As a direct result, organisational projects were delivered late and with significant cost overruns.

- In one large B2B sales organisation, the Sales Director had a large number of direct reports. While proficient in many aspects of his leadership behaviours, the quantitative survey clearly indicated poor scores in Clarity, Recognition and Involvement.

Simply, the Sales Director's reports felt there was insufficient time in which they could engage to learn about the organisation's intent and their contributory role, i.e. Clarity; there was insufficient time to talk about performance and gain a sense of discretionary review, i.e. Recognition; and they felt they were not a homogeneous Sales team, i.e. Involvement.

Job Completeness

- When a job is designed such that people experience job completeness, it means they have the opportunity to be involved in a range of activities rather than a 'fractionalised' experience, e.g. making Adam Smith's[35] pinheads.

The following anecdote is apposite.

"Waiter, there's bits in my omelette!"

Consider the production of omelettes and the process being sub-divided in to egg-cracker, egg whisker, omelette fryer, and omelette server. If the egg cracker doesn't crack the eggs carefully, the latter serves omelettes full of egg-shell to the customer. If there is no feedback loop, it is a recipe for disaster! (Sorry!)

A lack of Job Completeness often undermines the extent to which people experience Clarity in their organisation. The extent to which they are involved in only part of a process inhibits the development of their appreciation of how their contribution fits into the broader task deliverable, i.e. "I didn't realise egg-shell messes up the omelette". This is amply illustrated in many clerical and shop-floor roles.

We often observe poor Job Completeness scores in functional positions, e.g. Finance and HR management roles. These professionals complain they do not understand how their work is being utilised to best effect within their organisation.

We also see it in Sales organisations. While they interface with customers, they may have relatively little interaction with operational or marketing colleagues; indeed technology can exacerbate this by virtue of their submitting orders on-line, displacing previous telephone conversations. Many times we have observed weak scores in Job Completeness to render poor Clarity scores which, in performance outcome terms, causes effort to be misdirected to selling the least profitable products, rather than those products that fit most strategically with the overall direction of the business.

Put simply, a low Job Completeness score drags back Climate, which will have serious knock-on effects on bottom line. We have seen this so frequently, it is a no-brainer.

At the end of this Chapter, we provide a detailed Case Study considering how measurement across the elements of the Integrated Framework has a real and material impact upon it improving its performance. In this we see the effect that poor Job Clarity and Job Accountability scores had upon its Climate.

Processes and their link to Climate

Each group of individuals has its own way of working as a team. The different approaches reflect the balance between the way individuals might prefer to behave and the behaviours necessary for effective team working. This framework defines the processes that represent categories of group behaviour that are critical for success. For example:

- What processes prevail in terms of decision-making?

- Is decision-making an effective process within that particular group of people?

- Does decision-making receive the correct data at the right time?

- Is enough time spent in the analysis of problems?

- Does business planning holistically link the corporate plan to individuals' performance plans or is there no sense of association?

In terms of the framework, we identify thirteen critical processes that drive Climate. This framework is shown in Table 3.2. (a more detailed description is provided in Appendix 1). Put simply, if the process is delivered effectively in the organisation, it will drive the creation of a positive Climate. The reverse is true, too.

Table 3.2: THE FACTORS OF TEAM PROCESSES

FACTOR	MEANING
PLANNING	Well-established and effective planning processes are utilised, which clearly drive what is done through setting clear goals and objectives.
RELATIONSHIPS	There is sound, effective communication within teams and between teams. People consider there is mutual trust, which enables folk to be open with others and extend bi-lateral support. Overall, the team comes before the individual.
TEAM EFFECTIVENESS	The team comprises the appropriate mix of skills, knowledge and experience to effectively carry out its responsibilities. There is an effective performance management process in place, which is actively used so allowing the team and its members to know how it and they are performing. People have the opportunity to develop themselves.
PERFORMANCE	People know how decisions are made across the organisation and recognise the system to be effective rather than bureaucratic. Resources are applied to tasks in a manner that efficiently matches skill with task demand, which produces a high level of co-ordination and co-operation between team activities.

A summary of the correlations between these Processes and Climate is provided in Appendix 2.

Planning

- The more effective the planning process is in involving and engaging individuals, the clearer will be their sense of understanding of what is being set as corporate intent. Furthermore, they will appreciate how what they actually do is linked to this sense of direction.

  Fundamentally, planning in managerial 'ivory towers' does not help build Clarity, Autonomy nor, of course, Involvement. Where managers observe a low Clarity score, they need to put extra effort into planning in order to drive up this score.

We can do better than that!

In one client situation, the leadership team had started its planning process and outlined some performance goals. They decided to pull together a virtual team comprising a 'diagonal slice' across the business, representing all levels and functions. This team came up with a more ambitious plan than the leaders had produced, they had it accepted by their colleagues, and then went on to exceed the goals. This was in a quite heavily unionised environment, too. (The reference to Ricardo Semler made earlier is apposite here, too, in considering the very considerable degree to which an organisation's staff can be involved in the planning process.)

Communication

- The more effectively an executive team engages with itself and that of a range of colleague teams around the organisation, the greater will be the level of communication that prevails. We find that effective communication processes or systems build both Clarity and Autonomy.

  The greater the level of appreciation for what others are doing and why, the greater scope leaders have to make their own decisions and to implement ideas without reference because they will know intuitively how things will 'fit' into the overall scheme of things. If a team scores low in Autonomy (and resultant performance outcomes are poor), the remedy or fix is to tackle Communication.

Leadership Behaviours (of managers and managerial teams) and its link to Climate

Here are considered how managers or management teams use different behavioural approaches to pursue the various activities and objectives that are an integral part of their role. This can include establishing a sense of direction and purpose for the work that people do and the process of influencing an individual or group to capture their interest and buy-in to that, if you wish, 'vision'. It can also involve providing inspiration and enthusiasm for others through their behaviours in terms of sharing information and making available development.

These behaviours apply to the full range of interactions that managers have with their employees, colleagues, bosses, i.e. the most junior member of staff with their manager through to the Chief Executive with their Chairman, as well as investors, owners, customers and suppliers. This includes leadership from the perspective of a formal line management role, as well as more informal relationships.

In the context of the Integrated Framework, the leadership dynamic has a clearly critical effect on the Climate of any group or collection of individuals with whom the leader engages. Behaviours are a very significant part of this dynamic and, when delivered effectively, they can help create a performance-orientated Climate. Managers failing to create such a Climate cannot expect to see their people deliver comparable performance to organisations in which a more favourable Climate has been created.

Table 3.3 shows a summary of the Leadership Behaviour framework (a more detailed version is provided in Appendix 1), which is represented by six broad behavioural approaches, each of which comprises a number of subordinate measures. Again, we have assessed the correlations between these behaviours and the creation or formation of Climate within the organisation; a summary of these is provided in Appendix 2.

Table 3.3: THE FACTORS OF LEADERSHIP BEHAVIOUR

FACTORS	MEANING
DIRECTIONAL	Leaders consider what options the organisation has in the future and create a clear, unambiguous long-term direction for their enterprise. They then ensure all activities are co-ordinated and aligned to bringing about achievement of the selected direction.
ENGAGING	Leaders are able to win the commitment of others to contribute effort to achieving the long-term direction that has been set for the organisation. They build credibility and have presence when communicating; they are construed as being inspirational.
POSITIONAL	Leaders do their work and not that of their team members. They delegate effectively.
CONSTRUCTIVE	Leaders build long-term, open, constructive, mutually beneficial relationships. They do not avoid raising difficult issues with other people and will confront matters rather than allowing them to fester and, potentially, become corrosive. They manage performance, both good and bad.
DEMOCRATIC	Leaders share appropriate information with others, recognising that certain matters have to be kept confidential. They consult and seek the view and opinions of others, involving them in shaping their ideas and actively listen, respond and take action upon those suggestions.
DEVELOPMENTAL	Leaders provide timely, relevant and objective feedback to others so they know how they are performing. They consider that the development of others' potential and talent is a key responsibility of their job.

Here are some examples.

Directional behaviour

- The manager delivering Directional behaviour will spend time with his people establishing with them an understanding of the long-term direction of the business. He will encourage his team(s) to consider a range of options in terms of how they best add value to the overall business goals. Through his approach, the manager will ensure that the team's activities are well co-ordinated and linked in an effective way with each other and with other teams. This style of behaviour is also likely to be highly involving and engaging in order to get the best out of people.

  Our analysis shows a clear statistical correlation with the formation of a number of Climate dimensions. However, the real critical connect is with Clarity. In simple terms, if we measure Clarity as a low score we know that the manager needs to raise his game relating to the extent to which he is delivering effective Directional behaviour.

Positional behaviour

- Another interesting example is the dimension listed as Positional. A manager scoring highly in this dimension will be operating at the right strategic level, i.e. not doing the job below the level at which he is paid. He will also be highly successful in his delegation and will avoid the classic trap of a senior manager acting as a middle manager overly involved in the detail and working 18 hours per day.

  Positional leadership behaviour again drives and causes a wide range of Climate outcomes. Possibly the most interesting connection we observe with a low Positional score is low Challenge and Autonomy. In this context, the connection is entirely predictable when you work for a manager who essentially does your job for you; it is extremely difficult to feel energised or challenged, or to make decisions without reference to that person.

  These low Climate scores can be reversed when managers change their Positional game and can be further enhanced with the delivery of the Developmental behaviour, too. When the manager begins to deliver this particular behaviour, we tend to see an increase in Challenge, Clarity and Involvement.

Developmental behaviour

- Another dimension which has a strong effect upon Climate is that listed as Developmental. A manager scoring highly in this dimension will be spending time with his people, expending effort in giving them clear and timely feedback about their performance and providing them with tactical coaching input. He will also be engaging them in honest dialogue about their longer-term career aspirations and providing appropriate support and counsel.

  Developmental leadership, not surprisingly, has the most significant impact with Recognition where it contributes to building a meritocracy in which there is a clear distinction made between effort, outcome and reward. In other words, there is a sensible division of time between recognising and rewarding the best performers and addressing the short-comings of the poorer performers and dealing with the unwilling, i.e. differentiating between the 'can do', 'can't do' and 'won't do'. All too often in organisations that score poorly in Development and Recognition, the root cause lies in managers spending too much time with their least effective people. In our experience, this is especially the case in education and is a fundamental reason why schools do not enjoy positive Climates.

By addressing their own behaviours, leaders can have an immediate and positive impact upon Climate in their particular area of the organisation. To impact the other change levers probably necessitates leaders working collaboratively with their peers and colleagues.

It is important to recognise that this is NOT about motivating people; this is about building an environmental context, or Climate, in which people will motivate themselves.

An illustrative case study:

Measuring Climate and the change levers of the Leadership Dynamic

The previous section together with Chapter 2 have provided an overview of the Integrated Framework, which illustrates how Climate correlates with and drives organisations' bottom-line performance whatever sector they happen to operate in. The Framework clearly identifies how the *leadership dynamic* of Structure, Behaviour and Process links intricately with Climate. This framework, together with a survey methodology and benchmarking database, can be utilised in a highly practical way. The following case study provides an example of this type of intervention.

The case study involves an industrial manufacturing business and covers the period between the mid-to-late 1990s and mid-2000s. The background was that the business had changed its structure from a relatively independent set of geographical businesses into one global enterprise with a common brand and matrix structure. This was driven by the needs of the market-place. The incumbent CEO recognised the need to change how the organisation operated in this new business environment. Amongst other things it was deemed critical that the senior management population raised its level of capability in terms of Strategic Thinking and Relationship Building, together with lifting its capacity to provide leadership that unleashed the latent potential of its workforce.

The start of the process was a development programme involving the top 60 managers. The questionnaire suite referred to in Chapter 2, which underpins the Integrated Framework and provides a quantitative, benchmarked measure for each of the 60 individuals concerned, was employed. The survey required each of these managers' immediate reports to assess the following:

1. The leadership behaviour of the respective manager.

2. The team's evaluation of the Climate of the workgroup of which they were a part, and the overall organisation.

3. The effectiveness of the organisational structure and design seen from their own perspective.

4. The effectiveness of the Processes within their workgroup.

This set of 'mini-surveys' represented the opportunity for each manager to benchmark the effectiveness of the team he managed in the context of the Integrated Framework.

The next stage of the intervention was to run a series of four workshops, which were branded as 'Leadership for Organisational Improvement' (LOI™). In a practical sense, the LOI™ workshop provided a forum for each of the 60 managers to have the opportunity to review in a detailed manner all of the data relating to the components of the Integrated Framework arising out of the survey questionnaires completed by his team members. This gave all individuals the chance to identify the critical Climate issues, the business implications of those issues, and time to consider which to address and how. By having data relating to all aspects of their *leadership dynamic,* they could identify the causal reasons - be that their behaviour, structural weaknesses or process inefficiencies.

The basic question addressed was "What things do you as a manager need to turn on, turn off, change, modify etc. in order to drive an empowering organisational Climate?"

The workshop process as a whole was designed to represent a powerful and motivating learning experience for each participant, while concomitantly providing a clear focus to develop a change agenda that the senior management population would buy in to and pursue subsequent to participating in the diagnostic LOI™ workshop.

The management population defined for itself four levels of change agenda, which included:

1. Me as an individual.

2. Me as a leader of the team I manage.

3. We as a senior management team.

4. We as a business.

The survey process generated a wide range of different profiles across the 60 managers. However, it is fascinating to observe the aggregated results that were taken at the beginning of the intervention and to compare those with the aggregates lifted from the exact same survey process that was conducted four years later.

Figure 3.2 shows some of the results from the first measurement of Climate, Behaviour and Structure. The 0-100 scale represents a 'normative' comparison. If an individual's score is below 50, it means that more than half the database has a better score. An individual scoring over 50 has done better than half the database population. The database is an external, international benchmark comprising over 14,000 individual managers who have completed our surveys. Comparison is not restricted to the organisation being measured.

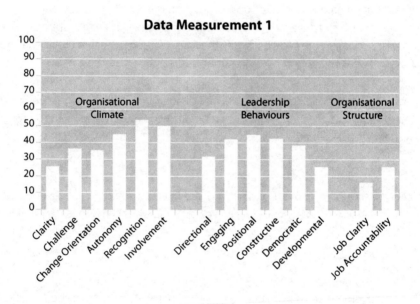

Figure 3.2

The data shows that, when first measured, the aggregated profile revealed a fairly moderate level of Climate but with a particularly poor picture revealed for Clarity and Change Orientation, i.e. each in the third quartile. The behaviour data highlights a particularly significant issue in terms of Directional, Democratic and Developmental behaviour scores (each around the 3rd/4th quartile). Particularly noticeable within the Structure profile are the dimensions of Job Clarity and Job Accountability, which were positioned at the 15th and 25th percentile respectively (notably, the first is markedly deep within the fourth quartile).

The top 60 participative population identified these as key issues that seemed to characterise most individuals' feedback and, when aggregated , showed particularly poor scores. The basic thinking was that these poor leadership scores, together with an absence of Job Clarity and Job Accountability were, (as it were) the main culprits underpinning the low scores in Climate of both Clarity and Change Orientation.

It was interesting to observe that underpinning the lack of Job Clarity and Job Accountability was a newly-formed matrix organisation that wasn't working effectively. At a simple and immediate level, this feedback provided powerful learning about how this management population needed to change the way it operated and functioned. It was quite revealing when, in one of the sessions, a senior director remarked, "I can't quite understand why Change Orientation is so low, because we are repeatedly *telling* [our italics] our people what needs to happen." 'Telling', of course, says it all. At a more profound level, as a result of identifying, assimilating, assessing and interpreting these statistical measurements, the senior management set out a series of specifically tailored interventions to address them.

This management population needed:

- To be more effective establishing direction with its staff.

- To deliver a greater level of Developing Others' behaviour together with a reduction of what was clearly perceived as a highly coercive style of behaviour.

- To achieve a more fluid and clear perspective in the business in relation to their matrix structure. The bottom line was that folk didn't quite appreciate where the buck stopped and started in terms of who was accountable for what.

Following a period of four years, the leadership population decided to run the LOI™ programme for a second time in order to measure the extent to which they had achieved improvement in the leadership dynamic and the resulting Climate outcome. These results are shown in Figure 3.3.

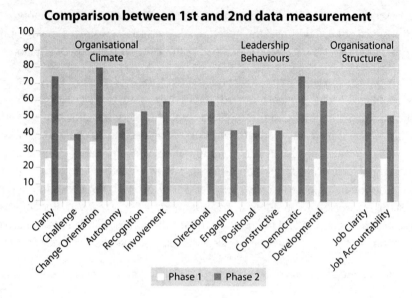

Figure 3.3

The data clearly indicate a substantial increase in both the Clarity and Change Orientation aspects of Climate, where these data have moved towards the top end of quartile 2 and into the upper quartile respectively.

A significant improvement in the Leadership Behavioural profile is shown, together with significantly improved perceptions of Job Clarity and Job Accountability.

In this study involving 60 managers, fully three-quarters of the population showed a measurable improvement in their leadership behaviour with no examples of behavioural deterioration.

As ever, we tried to establish the impact that this changing behaviour and enhanced Climate had in terms of bottom-line performance outcomes. We identified substantial improvements in terms of sales, speed and success of product development and customer satisfaction. It is, of course, impossible to prove in a real, scientific sense that these behavioural shifts absolutely underpinned these bottom-line gains. However, the evidence was very compelling and, more to the point, this senior management population did believe there were such clear and direct consequential relationships.

Through this intervention (and many others like it), I contend that the change in behaviour achieved by the management population, together with improvements in the workings of the matrix structure, caused people throughout the business to develop a far greater sense of what they were supposed to do and why, which was coupled with a greater sense of empowerment in terms of their preparedness to change. This shift in the Climate provided the firm foundation on which were built the improvements in sales performance, product development and customer satisfaction.

Conclusion

The Integrated Framework is underpinned by factual, statistical evidence derived from years of research and allied measurement coupled with practical consultancy that has occurred at all stages of the economic cycle more than one time around. The extensive database of individual managers' measurement reflects numerous organisational situations, ranging from multi-national conglomerates at one extreme to members of religious orders at the other (who also happen to be heads of schools, so are very much leaders in their own right), and from a multitude of international backgrounds. It is this wealth of information that provides the confidence to promulgate Climate to be the key driver of performance. Climate itself can be enhanced by addressing the components of each of the input change levers.

This work has proven the clear causal link that Climate is created by leaders and/ or managers - individually and, ideally, as a collective Executive, concentrating upon delivering effective behaviours and delivering these within a well-designed organisational structure augmented by efficient and effective processes. As a direct consequence, they will create a truly high-performance oriented Climate that can be sustained over a long period of time.

I started this chapter by posing the question about the conditions that need to be put in place in order to achieve sustainable high performance. Our Integrated Framework provides a critical solution to this problem by identifying the three change levers that drive Climate, which in turn drives performance.

- Climate drives bottom line performance.

- The three change levers of behaviour, structure and process drive Climate. Together they represent a powerful leadership dynamic.

- It is this dynamic that any successful leader needs to embrace and deliver.

- All of these factors can be measured in a benchmarked context and together represent a powerful balance sheet to drive a performance improvement agenda.

CHAPTER 4:

The behaviours and competencies that drive leaders and their organisations' performance

Our research underpinnings

During the 1980s, through intensive research with colleagues, I sought to identify and understand the behavioural characteristics that underpinned excellent performance. I wanted to understand how an individual needed to operate in order to deliver the type of leadership dynamic described in the previous chapter. Put another way, what is it that differentiates an outstanding from an average performer in terms of results delivery?

The research ranged across sectors, from the military to petro-chemical companies to pharmaceuticals to financial services to manufacturing to retail, and in all parts of the globe. As such, the behaviours identified in our work do cross cultural boundaries, although it must be said that there are subtle 'modes' that characterise their delivery in different parts of the world.

In addition to sectors and geographic regions, we have studied a wide array of functional groupings together with levels of operation ranging from the shop-floor to the Chief Executive. Table 4.1 shows a summary of some of the specific types of roles and groupings where research has been conducted.

The Chief Executive	The Food Scientist (chocolate to be precise!)
The Executive Director	
The CFO or FD	The Physicist
The HR Director	The Chemical Engineering Plant Manager
The CIO	The Chemical Plant Operator
The IT Director	The Contact Centre Team Leader
The Customer Service Director	The Contact Centre Advisor
The Corporate Banker	The Factory Supervisor
The Investment Fund Manager	The Mechanical and Electrical Engineer
The Trust Fund Manager	
The Accountant	The Vicar
The Sales Director	The Marketeer
The Salesman	Etc…
The Custodial Banker	
The Retail Banker	

Table 4.1

The format of the research approach involves conducting detailed interviews (in the blind) with a diverse population of individuals from the organisations with which we have worked. Some of these organisations have been actual companies, while some have been professional bodies. By 'in the blind', I mean that we knew nothing about the interviewees other than their first name and job title; we had no performance data, for instance. Interviewees describe recent achievements and provide a very detailed account of their career histories. The interviewee relates his narrative in relatively free-flow, with the interviewer probing to understand the detail of their behaviour in terms of thinking and actions at specific and real points in their story.

These interviews are tape-recorded and transcribed. The transcripts are then studied for evidence of behaviour. The evidence is then modelled in terms of a detailed written framework. At this point, additional data is obtained from the organisation in terms of performance outcomes for the individuals concerned, which gives the opportunity to correlate the framework data with bottom line deliverables.

One of the first studies conducted involved a large group of chemical plant managers. We expected that technical skill, knowledge and educational background would have a significant causal impact upon their level of performance in terms of the management of the plant. While it was clear that this level of knowledge was a critical requirement, i.e. in this case the whole population of managers needed this background, nevertheless it represented only a threshold requirement. What differentiated the outstanding and average performers was the behavioural framework articulated from the study. For example, we correlated educational performance, i.e. from their school and university qualifications, and failed to observe a statistically valid difference between outstanding and average performance in terms of this academic track record. When political efforts continue to increase the share of school-leavers that go on to tertiary education, it may appear heretical to remark that ultimately it is not educational qualification that is the primary factor in work-life performance. Yes, intelligence, or intellect, is needed but not necessarily as denoted by having a degree. In our analysis, graduates possessing different grades produce the same level of managerial and leadership performance (the scales, if tipped towards anyone, favoured those with 2:1s, which I attribute through phlegmatic experience to a simple syndrome of 'work hard, play hard'). We have also found this 'lack of correlation' with both individual contributors and knowledge-based roles and even within academic groups.

We found clear statistical evidence that it was behaviours, or *competencies*, which differentiated the poor, the average and the best performers. **It is not <u>what</u> someone does but <u>how</u> they do it.**

To this idea of behavioural competency is attached the following definition:

> *'A characteristic behaviour that can be shown to be associated with successful performance*[36]*.'*

An alternative definition would be:

> **'A way of behaving that is associated with obtaining successful results.'**

What do we actually mean by competency?

This chapter provides a thorough explanation to this question. In Table 4.2 we consider ten examples of competencies, which we have found to be particularly important behaviours for leaders to demonstrate.

Competency	Meaning
Initiative	Acts before being directed
Results Focus	Sets clear objectives for self and others in order to achieve an intended outcome
Concern for Impact	Modifies and adapts their approach with others in order to gain their commitment to a particular course of action
Inter-personal Awareness	Seeks to understand the concerns, drivers and motives of others
Tenacity	Demonstrates repeated effort to overcome obstacles and difficulties
Independence	Surfaces difficult issues with others in the face of clear opposition
Strategic Thinking	Develops clear vision for the future and the actions that need to be taken to make this reality
Conceptual Thinking	Thinks broadly about what is occurring in the world to help generate more creative and imaginative solutions to problems and issues

Concern (or Drive) for Excellence	Strives personally and with their team to identify and implement fresh, innovative ways of doing things
Strategic Influencing	Formulates a long-term change agenda and uses different influencing strategies to win commitment from others

Table 4.2

What do these competencies look like in real behavioural terms?

In the following illustrations, the italicised paragraph represents someone describing another's behaviour. The paragraph in upper-case explains why that description represents the particular behaviour.

Initiative

- *"When John started in the organisation in his new role, he recognised that there was a need for clear investment to be made in order to maximise the output of the plant. Off his own bat, he set about identifying the critical machinery that needed to be changed, and sought the requisite investment funding. Then he got the team together in order to deliver his required changes."*

  HERE JOHN DEMONSTRATES INITIATIVE BECAUSE HE DID SOMETHING WITHOUT BEING TOLD, WHICH ADDED VALUE AND RESULTED IN A POSITIVE OUTCOME FOR THE BUSINESS.

Results Focus

- *"I have known Stephen for many years and one thing you can rely on is his ability to deliver on time and on cost. The last time he took on a project, he established a clear plan which included mutually agreed objectives for each member of the project team. As well, he put in place contingencies in case things went wrong. He delivered a clear drive in order to make progress and aligned and co-ordinated everyone's activities to ensure that the job got done."*

STEPHEN DEMONSTRATED RESULTS FOCUS BECAUSE HE HAD A CLEAR OUTCOME IN MIND AND ESTABLISHED CLEAR OBJECTIVES FOR THOSE AROUND HIM. THIS BEHAVIOUR ENSURED AN EFFECTIVE, ON-TIME, ON-COST DELIVERY.

Concern for Impact

- *"Sometimes I am amazed with Jane's skill in getting people to see things her way. Last year she made a presentation to the engineering department about the need for them to align their activities carefully in terms of the organisation's marketing and sales activities. When she presented her argument she described it in such a way using facts and figures that it seemed to really appeal to those guys. She absolutely got them on board by how she made her input."*

JANE DEMONSTRATES HER CONCERN FOR IMPACT BY POSITIONING HER ARGUMENT IN A CERTAIN WAY THAT CAPTURED THE IMAGINATION OF THE ENGINEERS AND GOT THEM TO DO WHAT THE BUSINESS REQUIRED.

Inter-personal Awareness

- *"The person to go and ask about how the land lies is definitely Richard. He just seems to have a very good handle on what makes folk tick. The other week I had a conversation with him about one of our colleagues in the sales department. It was so useful to hear his insight about the person in question that I saw that person in a different light regarding their probable ulterior motives."*

RICHARD SHOWS HIS INTER-PERSONAL AWARENESS BY PROVIDING TO HIS COLLEAGUE A REALLY USEFUL INSIGHT ABOUT THE CONCERNS, DRIVERS AND MOTIVES OF ANOTHER PERSON.

Tenacity

- *"The thing about Sarah is that she never gives up. Indeed I don't know if you know this, but prior to joining the organisation she completed her Marketing Diploma which, in itself, is clearly an achievement. It was breathtaking to see her overcome balancing her work and home commitments on top of her college studies. She brings that same type of drive and determination to her current role. Indeed, she seems almost motivated when things get in the way."*

THIS HIGHLIGHTS SARAH'S TENACITY TO SHOW DRIVE AND ENERGY TO OVERCOME A DIFFICULT SET OF OBSTACLES AND SET-BACKS THROUGH REPEATED EFFORTS IN ORDER TO DELIVER THE PERFORMANCE OUTCOME.

Independence

- *"Jackie is a good member of the team to have on board. While she has a nice manner about her, what is really useful is that she lets you know what she really thinks. Last year, my FD and I were both really committed to a new line of funding we had agreed with our bankers about which we were soon to go public. In the light of this, Jackie suspected we would be pretty annoyed if she disagreed with us but she had the courage to raise her concerns with me in a very clear way. She did this firstly because she thought we were wrong and, secondly, because she thought it was an issue that could not go on unremarked. I must admit at the time I was irritated but soon after her intervention I began to realise what a great input she had made and how right she was."*

IT IS SO USEFUL FOR A CEO TO HAVE SOMEONE LIKE JACKIE IN THE TEAM. JACKIE IS PREPARED TO GIVE HER VIEWS ABOUT VERY CRITICAL ISSUES EVEN THOUGH SHE KNOWS IT IS RISKY FOR HER. IN THIS EXAMPLE, JACKIE'S TENDENCY NOT TO CURRY FAVOUR BUT TO SAY IT AS IT IS EVENTUALLY ENABLED THE CEO TO AVOID A DISASTROUS FUNDING DECISION.

Strategic Thinking

- *"When Joe was appointed as CEO, he recognised there was a lack of clarity about the type of business we were in. We needed to get back to our core skills of distributing a wide range of competitive retail banking products and services. He thought our acquiring a highly-regarded mortgage business would enhance our position in that area and also provide a range of other cross-selling opportunities. It would signal to the investment community our intent to lead consolidation in the retail banking. He used that thinking to drive our actions over the course of the next few years."*

JOE DEMONSTRATES HIS ABILITY TO DELIVER STRATEGIC THINKING THROUGH HIS CONSIDERATION OF THE REALITY OF THE MARKET PLACE, THE STRENGTHS AND WEAKNESSES OF THE ORGANISATION HE NOW LEADS AND THE DIRECTION AND SHAPE OF THE BUSINESS HE WANTS TO CREATE.

Conceptual Thinking

- *"When Sylvia was appointed as Director of Manufacturing, her first priority was to look at the issue of lost-time accidents and our poor safety performance, which had dogged many of our industrial units. She saw this as a serious issue both in terms of the well-being of our people as well as the substantial cost and reputation issues that safety represents. She really appreciated the threat to our business in terms of our licence to operate if we didn't improve matters. Additionally, she also recognised the broad range of causal factors that were likely to be underpinning the safety issues. Apart from inadequate technical know-how, she identified how a range of other features including leadership, employee relations issues, and our relationship with the local community were probably linked together as a conglomerate of factors that needed to be addressed."*

SYLVIA DEMONSTRATES HER CONCEPTUAL THINKING FIRSTLY BY RECOGNISING THE BREADTH OF THE ISSUE IN TERMS OF SAFETY AFFECTING THE BUSINESS'S ECONOMIC PERFORMANCE AND REPUTATION AND, SECONDLY, BY APPRECIATING THAT THE CAUSES OF THE ISSUES WERE NOT DOWN TO SIMPLE, UNILATERAL FACTORS BUT WERE, IN FACT, MUCH MORE CONVOLUTED AND RESULTED IN A FORM OF CULTURE MALAISE THAT UNDERMINED SAFETY PERFORMANCE: SHE SAW THE BIGGER PICTURE AND THE INTER-LINKAGES.

Concern (or Drive) for Excellence

- *"Paul is probably the best manufacturing manager I have worked for. From the minute I joined the organisation he was deeply energised to improve the standards, procedures and systems that we used. He was always encouraging us to consider best practice, to benchmark our performance outside the organisation and to seek to improve the manner in which we operated. His approach was relentless and I must say the outcome of his behaviour as a leader was to truly raise the standards of how we operated."*

PAUL DEMONSTRATES CONCERN FOR EXCELLENCE BY ENCOURAGING HIS STAFF TO CONTINUE TO SEEK TO IDENTIFY AND INTRODUCE ONGOING IMPROVEMENTS TO THE ORGANISATION'S SYSTEMS AND PROCEDURES THAT EXIST WITHIN THE REMIT OF HIS ROLE.

Strategic Influencing

- *"Mark saw himself as a leader of change and I can remember when he joined us that he had a clear view about what needed to change and improve over the course of the next few years. The key point, however, was that he really applied a broad range of influencing tactics and styles to bring all the various parties on board to his view of things. He was no 'one trick pony' in terms of the manner in which he engaged with all the different people. In so doing, he won the commitment of these people to his long-term objectives."*

MARK DEMONSTRATES HIS ABILITY AS A STRATEGIC INFLUENCER BY FIRST OF ALL HAVING A VIEW ABOUT WHAT NEEDS TO CHANGE IN THE MEDIUM TO LONGER TERM, I.E. BEYOND TWO TO THREE YEARS. HE RECOGNISED THAT THE NEED TO GET PEOPLE ON BOARD WOULD ONLY BE ACHIEVED BY DEPLOYING A RANGE OF DIFFERENT INFLUENCING TACTICS IN ORDER TO BUILD COMMITMENT.

Strategic Influencing is a critical behaviour for senior leaders to master but one that we see occurring infrequently. Strategic Influencing is far more sophisticated than, say, the behaviour of Rational Persuasion, where a very fact-based approach is made to win an argument. However, if the other person is not fact-orientated himself, it is entirely feasible that he will be 'turned off' by such a black and white submission. Strategic Influencing is also more to do with winning buy-in to significant change than simply acting in the right manner for a given situation, which is what the behaviour of Concern for Impact considers.

These are simple examples of 'competencies in action'. They underpin the delivery of successful outcomes. They represent behaviours that, when delivered by managers, lead to a much greater chance of them 'upping their game'. As will be explored later, the extent to which an individual can effectively combine all these distinctive behaviours will be reflected in an ever increasingly rounded leadership contribution. For example, in the Independence example, we saw Jackie raising a sensitive and difficult issue with her CEO. If this behaviour is combined, as it were, with Concern for Impact it will be even more effective. The 'what' is said is wedded to the 'how' it is said.

To make the point absolutely clear, it is the frequency by which these behaviours are observed that we have found to correlate statistically with outcomes such as improvements in:

- Sales performance

- Customer satisfaction (as indicated in Chapter 1, that could be students in an educational institution)

- Business growth

- Product development

- Number of successful patents registered

- Efficacy of the marketing campaign

- Project completion etc.

Competency types

There are broadly three types of competencies that our studies have revealed.

Distinguishing competencies

- These refer to behaviours that characterise truly superior performance. If we analyse the behaviour of a group of superior performers and compare them with those doing the same job but to a lower standard, i.e. measured in terms of outcome effectiveness, we see that the key to their superior performance lies in the strength and consistency of their delivering certain competencies.

Threshold competencies

- These represent the behaviours that are a fundamental requirement of the role. Non-delivery would represent extremely poor performance. For example, when a waiter takes orders inaccurately the wrong meals get served. This lack of accuracy or 'Attention to Detail' behaviour would be disastrous. However, having accuracy as a behaviour does not make you an outstanding waiter; it is simply a threshold requirement below which the waiter cannot afford to operate if he wishes to be considered as any way half-decent.

Functional competencies

- By functional, we mean a particular behavioural attribute that has a very specific requirement in a certain role.

  For example, it is critical for a Chief Executive to establish the long-term direction and shape of the organisation for which he is accountable. For a Chief Executive, therefore, the competency of *Strategic Thinking* has particular functional relevance.

  For the Brand Manager who is required to bring to his work highly creative and novel thinking together with the ability to see connections between sometimes apparently disparate factors, the competency of *Conceptual Thinking* will be of critical importance in the role.

For the manufacturing Production Manager, a key requirement is the ability to drive a continuous level of performance improvement, always endeavouring to achieve more from less, together with the ability to bring in best practice whenever possible. A particularly important competency in this regard is called *Drive for Excellence*, which concerns delivering high quality outputs and findings ways to make them even better.

Functional competencies can actually be both threshold and distinguishing. For example, Strategic Thinking in a senior management position, e.g. a functional head, is likely to be observed as a significant distinguishing competency. However, for a CEO of a major plc, it is likely to be merely threshold behaviour. In other words, to operate at this level it is vital to have this behaviour; not having it could be abject failure.

At a fundamental level, therefore, a threshold competency is delivered by both the superior and average performer. A distinguishing competency is delivered more frequently by the superior performer.

When observing the behaviours of average and outstanding performers there is an absolute, statistically significant difference when you compare the frequency of delivery of observed behaviours and performance outcome; the outstanding performer delivers the distinguishing behaviours more frequently and to greater potency.

There are additional nuances that need to be considered in terms of strength and frequency of delivery of particular competencies, which adds further substantive means to assessing a manager's performance as superior or average, i.e. there is a measurement calibration.

Often, one would expect to see certain competencies demonstrated by people operating at different organisational levels. For instance, if an individual occupies a senior role, it is likely that he will be expected to do work of a more strategic nature than if he were in a more junior post. This will affect the extent to which, say, Strategic Influencing should be witnessed in the way he operates.

Other behaviours reflect a level of complexity, e.g. the scope of change being administered. In this case, therefore, the degree of Initiative displayed would be greater, while some behaviours are not related to grade or inherent complexity of task. They represent an increasing strength of effectiveness of overall delivery, e.g. Inter-personal Awareness or Independence.

The behaviours described earlier in this Chapter represent just some of the 25 behaviours (a summary of which is provided in the Appendices) we have identified through research to be the critical and crucial behavioural ingredients of successful leadership and management delivery. In very many different contexts and situations, each of these behaviours has been demonstrated to be a significant differentiator between average and outstanding performance. Obviously, which competencies are the most important will depend on the particular role and the level of role, and whether they are considered distinguishing or threshold.

In terms of growing one's proficiency in delivering competencies as opposed to skills, far more effort is required to accomplish this; skills are more easily trainable than competencies. While it is admirable to seek to deliver the optimum level in all of the behaviours, this is not realistic. Both I and any of my colleagues have yet to meet a leader who scores 'top marks' across all behaviours. Nevertheless, the better an individual can consistently deliver strongly in as many behaviours as possible, the more superior will be their performance.

Returning to the study of chemical plant managers mentioned a few pages back, I found that those plants that had good Health and Safety records and no pollution incidents were efficient and productive; enjoyed good industrial (or employee) relationships; saw more implementation of innovative ideas to improve operations; and were led by managers who consistently delivered significantly more examples of these behaviours than those managing averagely-performing plants. A higher level of capability in delivering the behavioural component of the *leadership dynamic* resulted in a far healthier Climate, and markedly better performance.

From our research and client engagements, we have developed a range of competency frameworks for different organisations and types of job. From that body of data a 'generic framework' was developed, which is shown in Table 4.3.

LEADERSHIP DOMAIN	COMPETENCY CATEGORY	INDIVIDUAL COMPETENCIES
Develops Vision and Purpose	THINKING	Strategic Thinking
		Customer Understanding
		Analytical Thinking
		Conceptual Thinking
		Forward Thinking
Gains Organisational Commitment	INFLUENCING	Strategic Influencing
		Rational Persuasion
		Relationship Building
		Interpersonal Awareness
		Concern for Impact
		Developing Others
Achieves Organisational Outcomes	ACHIEVING	Results Focus
		Concern for Excellence
		Initiative
		Critical Information Seeking
		Attention to Detail
		Thoroughness
Manages Self	SELF MANAGEMENT	Independence
		Tenacity
		Flexibility
		Self Development
		Organisational Commitment
		Self-belief
		Self-control

Table 4.3

In Appendix 3, there are some examples of formal definitions of these behaviours.

The framework consists of four 'clusters' of behaviours. Three of these clusters relate directly to three critical areas of activity in which leaders are engaged. A fourth behavioural cluster relates to how an individual governs himself. See Figure 4.1.

Leadership Activities and Their Mapped Behaviours

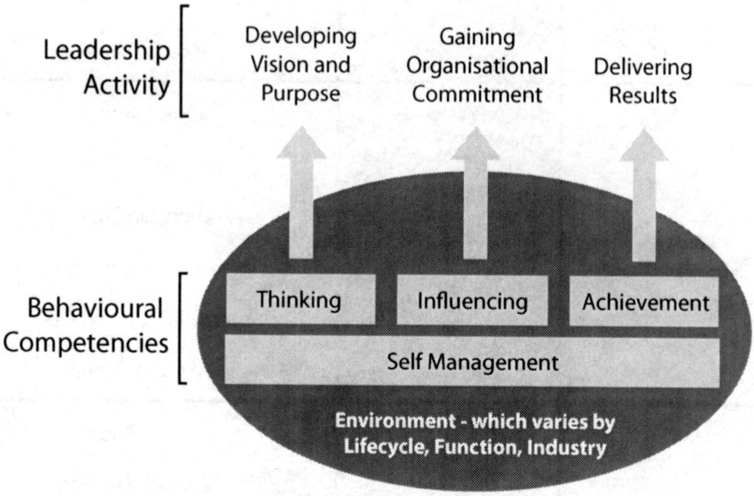

Figure 4.1

More fully, these activities and behaviours relate to the following:

• **Developing Vision and Purpose - Thinking**

This domain of leadership is concerned with managing the direction of the company, business unit, department or team within the context of its market sector and its external and internal customers.

The critical competencies in this domain all concern Thinking, i.e. what goes on in our heads. It covers our ability to analyse and make sense of the issues we face, to understand our customers, and to plan for the long term.

If you wish, this can be construed as 'visioning'.

• Gaining Organisational Commitment - Influencing

This domain is concerned with that part of leadership which is so crucial yet is often given insufficient attention, i.e. getting people's buy-in to the changes associated with the vision and required way forward. We seldom achieve much on our own. Influencing describes the way we engage and develop relationships with others, our sensitivity to them, balanced by our ability to persuade and influence. It also includes our role in the development of others, together with our capacity to think about and deliver complex change.

The successful leader will build a high degree of commitment from people at all levels in the organisation, and also from appropriate external bodies. For instance, a Team Leader within a Contact Centre of a bank or major utility could invoke change across the organisation by influencing upwards, laterally, downwards and out to external suppliers, e.g. manufacturers of call routing systems, and delivers exceptional sales and service by virtue of the way he develops his team members.

The simple construct here is of 'networking'.

• Delivering Results – Achieving

Achieving covers our ability individually and through others to complete tasks, deliver excellence, initiate and implement new ideas and improvements in the organisation, and acquire and assimilate information to understand what is happening and why.

The behaviour of high-performing leaders is characterised as being focused on delivering results that in the short-term represent clear, explicit steps towards the attainment of the longer term business vision.

The baseline is that of 'realising' (the vision) (some managers refer to 'execution').

The fourth cluster of behaviours relates to how the manager manages himself and contributes significantly to his effective delivery of the other competencies and, thereby, the overarching activities for which he is held accountable. We call this fourth cluster of behaviours, 'Self-Management'.

- **Self-Management**

  Behaviours in this cluster provide the foundation on which excellent performance is built. It describes our ability to control and develop ourselves, our commitment to the goals and values of our organisation, our ability to think and act independently and to be responsive to change.

  The successful leader demonstrates a determination to succeed whatever the obstacles. This is supported by a propensity to stand up for one's ideas in the face of opposition, and an ability to see the value of alternative viewpoints.

  The outstanding leader will also have a clear long-term vision for his own professional and personal development that he is working towards.

The competency frameworks we design and help organisations put into practical application indisputably help individuals to assess and improve their own behavioural performance and, as leaders and managers, that of others, too.

From our substantive evidence, it is clear that the manager who effectively delivers the appropriate mix of behaviours will be the one who is most successful in delivering the 'leadership dynamic' described in Chapter 3. He will ensure that the design of his organisational structure meets the demands of its customers and will possess the drive and imagination to continually upgrade processes so they work effectively. Most obviously and fundamentally, he will possess the required wherewithal to deliver those leadership behaviours that we observed in Chapter 3.

Our frameworks provide a practical, usable common language that can be used in feedback and coaching sessions, which will be understood by both the coach and the person being coached. In so doing, this is more likely to result in action being taken that will cause performance to improve. There is a mutual understanding of the specificity of what is being talked about, i.e. "When you interject in meetings, it is very abrupt. Consider last week…" What is being considered is explicit and tangible; it is neither nebulous nor ethereal.

How do competencies fit with other personal characteristics?

Behavioural competency fits into a framework of personal characteristics that relate to how individuals develop and operate as human beings. Whilst not wanting to wade too deeply into the waters of psychological theory, it will be useful to position competency alongside these other features, which are used to describe people's characteristics.

Skills

- This term should be used to describe an ability or skill to carry out a specific technical or management process successfully, i.e. he is a competent cook, he is competent at negotiating, he is competent at implementing a new computer system, he is competent at designing product packaging.

  In this sense, it is essential to recognise, therefore, that 'processes' such as sales or selling, negotiation, change management, even leadership, are not behaviours or competencies. Rather they are the critical outcomes that are required in the job and represent an individual's tasks or objectives. Being effective is determined by a range of critical behaviours or behavioural competencies.

  ### "Romeo, Romeo, wherefore art thou, Romeo?"

  Consider an actor or musician who may very skilled at learning the script or the score. However, if he does not convey the underlying emotion containing the oratory or music, his performance falls far short of what the audience expects to see. Behaviour is the differential.

  Benjamin Zander, the principal conductor of the Boston Philharmonic, was remarked to have said, "When the audience comes to see my orchestra, I don't want them to think we have only played the notes off the page. I want them to leave the auditorium *molecularly reconstructed* by virtue of the passion we put into our playing."[37]

Skills are often learned, technical abilities, including those for which we show no real aptitude, e.g. using a PC, but which we have to develop to deal with the demands of modern-day life.

Other skills may be seen as more innate and stem from our physical or psychological make-up, e.g. we can run fast, we can repair intricate devices, or we can remember people's faces and names. Perhaps not unsurprisingly, we often find that some of our basic skills are aligned with motives or values (see below) because we tend to be better at those things we care about, are interested in and help us achieve our goals.

In Appendix 4, we provide a simple exercise for you to consider that is designed to help you understand this critical distinction between competences, i.e. skills, and competencies, i.e. behaviours.

• Traits and Predispositions

These are characteristics of our personality, e.g. being extrovert or a very sociable person as opposed to one who is more introvert and quiet. Clearly, such traits will affect how we behave. Traits are frequently *measured* using questionnaire-based assessment tools, which generate outputs set against definitional frameworks, which enable individuals to describe their own traits as well as those of other people. In so doing, each has a better understanding of himself and of others.

• Motives

We touched on motives in Chapter 1 and will return to the topic in Chapter 6. One definition of motives is:

'A recurrent concern for a goal stake which energises and orientates behaviour.'

Thus, when we are hungry we seek something to eat which, once satisfied, removes the motive to do so until we become hungry again.

Earning money is another motive; it is one reason why we turn up at work every day although, at a higher level, we are motivated by our ambitions, our desire to build harmonious relationships, and our sense of striving to achieve. Motives drive us and affect the priority we give to the different things we do.

• Values

These refer to our beliefs and the concepts or principles that that we regard as inviolate. Examples include equality, truth, honesty, integrity, openness and family life. Within organisational, business life, we include concepts such as customer sovereignty and product or service excellence.

Like motives, we are not necessarily fully aware of what we value – until it is gone. Motives are different from values in that they represent deep level drivers, which often underpin the behaviours, or activities, we enjoy and feel 'truly motivated' to engage with. Values, on the other hand, represent deep-seated beliefs that tend to be reflected in the behaviours and activities which we feel are important and believe in.

Figure 4.2 contrasts the difference between motives and values. However, both are important factors which influence behaviour and, therefore, drive competencies; yet, while they are important, they are not what we mean by competencies.

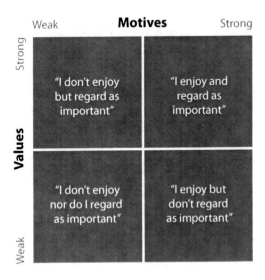

Figure 4.2

- ## Knowledge

We spend most of our childhood and adolescence acquiring knowledge about the world. Through the concept of life-long learning, we continue to acquire knowledge throughout adulthood, too, and, if nothing else, it helps us cope with the pace of change in the world around us. Acquiring new knowledge through conscious learning helps us to achieve our aims, i.e. "I need to be able to interpret financial data." This can be learned and mastered.

What we know obviously affects how we operate. But the 'outcome' of knowledge is not what we mean by competencies. In our definition of behavioural competency we would suggest that knowledge is both acquired more quickly and utilised more efficiently if the individual possesses and demonstrates the appropriate behavioural competencies. For example, if the individual is a highly results-focused person, demonstrates the behaviour of tenacity or drive and also combines this with very good analytical thinking, he is more likely to succeed in assimilating a detailed knowledge-based curriculum to a high standard than an individual who does not demonstrate these behaviours.

- ## Experience

While knowledge may be gained from books and observation, experience relates to the things that have actually happened to us. Experience tends to be a tough teacher and we often learn most from events that we would rather not have experienced, e.g. touching the hot stove as a child, saying something inappropriate in a meeting. The old adage, "You learn from your mistakes" is entirely apposite.

Experience teaches us about risk and about the need to plan.

The fit between competency and personality, skills and knowledge

These various factors of skills, traits, motives etc. are connected in quite complex ways. Taken together, they provide useful clues as to why we behave in the way we do. However, for people working in organisations, there is more than enough to do without trying to psycho-analyse ourselves and our colleagues.

In a great deal of recent literature and in many of the organisational competency frameworks we have reviewed, competency is applied as a catch-all phrase for many of the attributes we have just considered. This is an ineffective economy and taxonomy. It causes only confusion and ambiguity. By adhering to the purity of the original thinking about the concept of 'behavioural competency', we dispense with the confusion.

In my mind, competency provides the best means of describing what people do because it is observable and measurable. Stand in front of a group and ask what you are doing, and the group can respond with tangible descriptions. Ask why, and they can only guess because they cannot 'see' your personality, although they could guess.

Considering other measurement calibrations, it is quite clear that each is distinctive and does not get applied to another. For instance, measuring linear distance is done in kilometres and metres (miles and yards for someone of my age!). To measure capacity, it is litres (or gallons). This applies equally to competencies: they are behavioural, nothing else!

This does NOT mean we cannot change and improve our delivered behaviours. Figure 4.3 shows how competency fits alongside the concepts we have just explained.

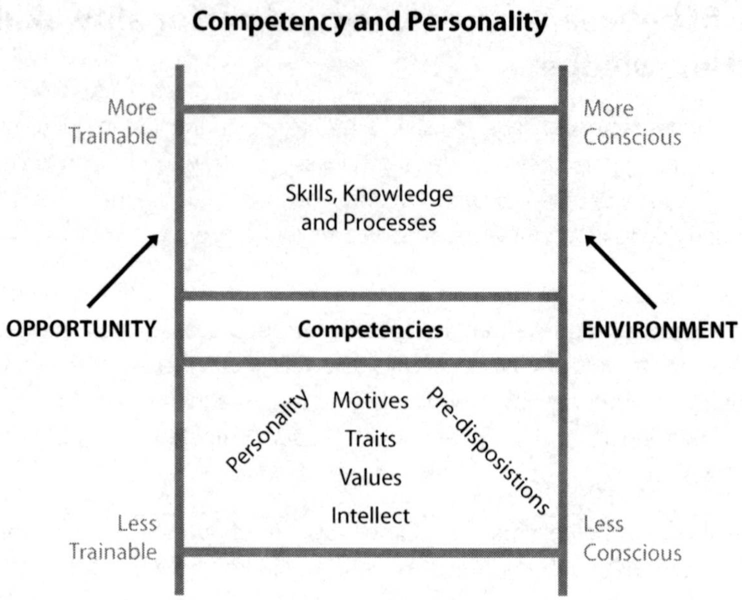

Competency and Personality

Figure 4.3

In summary, Figure 4.3 demonstrates:

- Traits, motives and values are key drivers of an individual's character and, thereby, can influence the competencies they are likely to deliver. A person's intellectual capacity will also influence the competencies they deliver.

- These competencies influence the effectiveness by which people deliver their skills and knowledge in the work-place.

- The delivery of a particular competency will also be affected by the style or Climate provided by the environment in which they operate, e.g. 'Initiative' is unlikely to emerge in a heavily rule-bound environment or where the leader is highly coercive.

- Competency delivery can also be influenced by the opportunity that the individual has had or that the organisation provides. For example, if the individual is employed in a highly structured, number-crunching type of role, he probably won't get the opportunity or exposure that enables him to deliver a strategic contribution.

- Individuals are more aware, or conscious, of their skills than they are of their competencies, motives, traits and values.

In other words, people tend to be aware of their ability to ride a fast motorbike safely, but tend not to wake up in the morning and think, "I haven't done any *conceptual thinking* today; I must do something about that".

This issue of consciousness or lack of consciousness about competencies, motives, traits and values raises the critical value of feedback.

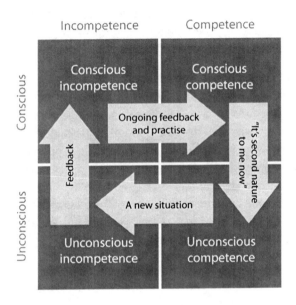

Figure 4.4

Figure 4.4 demonstrates how good feedback enables people to become 'consciously incompetent', i.e. individuals know what they are not good at as opposed to being entirely in the dark about certain aspects of their performance. Further effective feedback and coaching should enable the individual to master delivery of a competency in a conscious manner.

Over time, an individual can become 'unconsciously competent', i.e. things become second nature, which could lead to someone being blasé or complacent. However, the volatility of most organisational environments, driven by the dynamics of their market-place, tends not to provide too much time to bask in such glory because things have moved on and additional conscious effort is required.

Moving into a new role, a new environment or situation could result in the individual becoming 'unconsciously incompetent' until such time as he receives some meaningful and pertinent feedback.

Conclusions

I have commented that management processes such as leadership, negotiation and change management, while being important factors within the managerial space, are not just behaviours or competencies.

The definition of competencies that are applied throughout our methodologies relates to specific and detailed descriptions of a range of behaviours, some of which we have described above. Collectively, these underpin critical managerial processes and affect how well they are performed. This may sound somewhat academic, but we know from our practical experience supporting organisations applying competencies in recruitment, performance management and learning and development contexts, that they do indeed have the single most significant impact upon leadership performance than any of the other characteristics that can be brought to bear by an individual. A behavioural focus and style of definition makes for a much more practical application.

An example of this can be neatly illustrated with reference to the process of negotiation. What makes for an average performer? For example, it could be due to low Independence; there is an inability to raise a difficult issue, i.e. to ask for agreement to the deal, to raise the price, to resist reducing the price. On the other hand, it could be due to poor Critical Information Seeking, where the particular negotiator has not really comprehensively evaluated all of the information to hand and sought further information. Another issue could be that the negotiator may simply be weak in terms of his Interpersonal Awareness, and has failed to determine the motives of those with whom he is negotiating or to read effectively their non-verbal signals. (Consider a simple personal issue when you go to buy something, e.g. a car. The good salesperson can read whether you are prepared to buy or walk away. What they then do is more a matter of effective Concern for Impact, of course.) In a change management scenario, the average performer may exhibit weak Forward Thinking, poor Relationship Building, Developing Others, Results

Focus or Tenacity.

Hopefully, the point has been irrefutably made that these competencies, when delivered as a total, inter-dependent, inter-reliant set, collectively underpin the delivery of successful organisational outcomes. If we reconsider the Integrated Framework (see Figure 4.5), competencies are positioned as the 'raw ingredients' of the Leadership Behaviours that help drive Climate.

The Glowinkowski Integrated Framework

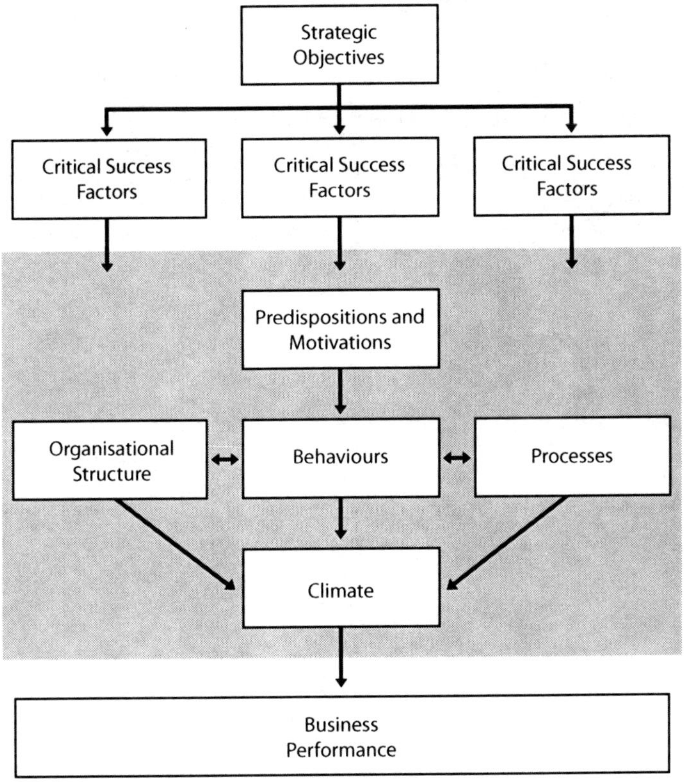

Figure 4.5

Leaders who bring the right mix or blend of behavioural competencies ensure that an effective organisational structure is put in place and, through evolution, remains fit for purpose. They will also establish efficient processes that undergo continual review and refinement to improve their effectiveness. They will have a greater capacity to deliver across the board of the six leadership behaviours defined within the Integrated Framework. There is, therefore, an inter-dependability between the three 'change levers' that drive Climate (hence the lateral arrows in the illustration).

From my work, therefore, there is compelling evidence that it is the behavioural competencies that underpin outstanding performance rather than some of the other factors that are traditionally considered in selection criteria.

To conclude, at the risk of repeating myself but on the basis this is the most crucial of points:

Competencies are entirely behavioural; anything else and you are not considering competencies!

They are the critical ingredients that underpin effectiveness in managing the leadership dynamic which drives Climate and performance.

They differentiate high from average performance in terms of the achievement of successful outcomes.

CHAPTER 5:

Why we do what we do: how the concept of
Predispositions helps our understanding

In the previous chapter, I provided a detailed account of the types of actual, delivered behaviours, or competencies, which underpin outstanding performance in a managerial role, so enabling delivery of the leadership dynamic that builds a high-performance Climate. In this chapter, I want to consider the factors that may contribute to the manager delivering such behavioural competencies. At one level, it is obvious there are a range of organisational factors, including Climate itself, which influence the degree to which a manager can practise these behaviours, i.e. a low Change Orientation in Climate will probably subdue a manager's ability to deliver Initiative particularly strongly. The rules and protocols of the organisation's culture may be similarly limiting.

From the perspective of thinking about an individual, it is particularly interesting to consider which deeper-seated personal characteristics may be at force in providing the 'raw material' to deliver a particular behaviour. Another way of putting this is to ask the question, "Why do people do what they do?" I am not asking this question from the perspective of motivation, i.e. doing things because there is an inherent need or because they are enjoyable but, instead, to consider the matter in the context of "What is it that causes people to behave in a certain way because it is 'easier' to deliver certain competencies than others?"

For instance:

- Why do some people find it easier to generate creative ideas?

- Why do some people find it easier to work to targets and deadlines?

- Why do some people find it easier to engage with others?

The corollary, therefore, is that some people find it a real, personal challenge to deliver certain behaviours in certain situations.

This chapter explores the idea of **Predispositions**, or preferred behaviours. Essentially, this chapter discusses an aspect of personality in the guise of a set of vital factors that may influence significantly how an individual delivers the behaviours discussed in the preceding chapter and, thereby, defines his performance as a manager.

What are Predispositions?

There is an immense array of literature written about personality. A critical 'tap root' into the world of this science is provided by the work of Paul Costa, Robert

McCrae and Oliver John who, in various combinations, produced some seminal material during the 1980s. Their work coined the 'Big 5 Trait Theory of Personality'[38]. Also recognised is the contribution made in influential research from Kurt Lewin, Raymond Cattell, Hans Eynsenck, Richard Boyatzis and David McClelland[39]. Indeed, as well as this academic literature, many managers have experienced completing and receiving feedback from personality questionnaires such as Myers-Briggs or OPQ.[†]

Predispositions represent the stable characteristics, or traits, of an individual. They can be seen as representing the nature of 'who we are' as individuals and can be thought of as our *preferred* or *natural* approach to addressing problem-solving and managing social interactions. Traits are a relatively fixed aspect of our underlying personality, e.g. the conscientious seven year old will still be conscientious at 27, 47 and 67.

Predispositions can influence or drive delivered behaviour, but they are not necessarily the same thing as delivered behaviour. For instance, an individual with a low preference (Predisposition) for detailed, methodical work can often perform highly effectively when this approach is required by the task in hand, e.g. the creative marketer often has to handle the matter of setting well-defined, unambiguous terms and conditions, or agreeing financial budgets. In a social context, an individual may be required to be friendly and outgoing yet, in reality, their Predisposition could be one of being cool and aloof.

In these simple examples, people are delivering behaviours required by the situation. In everyday life, whether we like it or not, we are required to deliver behaviour that is not necessarily reflective or congruent with our natural approach; we have to act out of character. The behaviours described in the previous chapter can be learned, so that when they are delivered it is done so more consciously and, thereby, effectively. Where such delivery is simply 'coping behaviour', this is more taxing. Over time, this can prove stressful and debilitating resulting in poorer performance being contributed. Indeed, very early research work conducted by the author in liaison with Cary Cooper[*] highlighted a key cause of stress to be related to delivering 'coping behaviour'.

---

† Myers-Briggs Type Indicator was devised during the Second World War by Katherine Cook Briggs and Isabel Briggs Myers, mother and daughter and the first questionnaire was published in 1962. Costa and McCrae, amongst others, have criticised its validity. OPQ is one of the world's best known personality questionnaires and is produced by SHL.

* Cary Cooper is regarded as one of the world's leading experts on stress and its causation in organisations. Steve Glowinkowski and Cary Cooper produced a paper entitled, Managers and Professionals in Business/Industrial Setting: The Research Evidence in 1987, which was published in the Journal of Organisational Behaviour.

So, Predispositions are defined as reflecting the nature of 'who we are' and how we 'prefer' to operate. It is important to appreciate that this is in a trait sense rather than a belief or values sense – see below.

> **Exercising choice**
>
> In facing a choice about whether to go to a business meeting or visit an ailing relative, traits and values will affect the decision made. While the business meeting may be something an individual wishes to go to because he 'prefers' to be in that sort of situation, it may well be that he visits the relative because that is considered 'the right thing to do'.

Preferred versus delivered behaviours

As managers, the difference between Predisposition and delivered behaviour can be considered to be the extent to which we have to deliver behaviour that is neither preferred nor natural but is, nevertheless, required by the task or situation.

Having a deep appreciation and understanding of our Predispositions can be extremely helpful in terms of people gaining an understanding as to why they do what they do and, also, why they feel as they do about certain activities. Such understanding and awareness provides a robust platform on which to base management development activity relating to learning how to deliver 'out of character' behaviours, i.e. effectively delivering behaviours that are different from Predispositions; in other words, 'to do well what we are not good at'. It is, of course, eminently sensible for people to play to their strengths. However, there is probably no occupation on earth, particularly at a senior level, where we can be 'naturally excellent' in every aspect of the requirements of the role. Therefore, you can play to your strengths all you like but no role in the universe allows you to ignore your gaps.

Kurt Lewin, mentioned earlier, posited that Actual Behaviours are a function of personality, i.e. Predisposition, and the situation in which they are delivered. This can be described as 'behaviour being a function of the person times the situation' or, in the following manner, which looks a little like a mathematical formula:

$$B = f(P \times S)$$

or, if you prefer

Behaviour = a function of Personality x Situation

More often than not, an individual delivers a behaviour that is natural to him, i.e. is 'driven' to act in a manner afforded by his Predispositions. However, employing organisations 'pay' for behaviour that is required by the task or situation rather than what the individual prefers through his natural character or predisposition.

The more an individual appreciates his predispositional make-up, the greater the opportunity provided to that individual to choose to start learning to be effective in delivering alternative behaviours. It is analogous to increasing the number of tools in the tool box. If you wish, personality is akin to an adjustable wrench: there is a degree of movement there to help it deal with some situations but nothing beats having a comprehensive array of single-sized spanners, which can be used in many more situations. A couple of examples from the author's own experiences merit mention.

Predispositions and delivered behaviours

One Executive client is more predisposed to keep her own company than to engage with other people. So after a lengthy discussion with a client, she wants some time to herself. As a result, the natural inclination is to get out and away from the meeting venue. It is not instinctive behaviour to pop her head into the offices of other people she knows in that building. Exercising this Predisposition is not conducive to building business. Her learned behaviour, however, predisposes her to say, "Hello", and so provides the gambit for further business development conversations to occur.

Another manager is more naturally an engaging and outspoken individual. He finds it hard to shut up which, at times, has seen him say the wrong thing at the wrong time, e.g. dealing with profaning, abusive customers is no time to 'fight back'. He has learnt to exercise the 'two ears, one mouth' rule in his engagement style in terms of the ratio of listening to speaking.

As an example of a trait being long-standing, this manager told me that as a child he was often chided by his parents and teachers for "not engaging his brain before opening his mouth".

Describing Predispositions

In academic literature, many of the terms, or labels, used to describe facets of personality are quite harsh. For instance, being described as 'neurotic' carries negative connotations. It is considered a pejorative term. I wanted to find a means of describing Predispositions in a non-pejorative manner. Any particular Predisposition can have both a positive and a negative impact in terms of potential behavioural outcome. For example, a socially engaging/talkative Predisposition will serve well in situations that require communication and active interaction. On the other hand, that same Predisposition could be highly negative in a different context such as carrying out work requiring individual concentration when a quieter, more hushed situation is needed. Also, a detail-conscious Predisposition works well when conducting meticulous engineering work or financial or scientific analysis but may be less appropriate when thinking 'blue sky'.

As indicated earlier, Predispositions are considered to be relatively stable aspects of an individual's personality. Of course, an astute individual will learn to deliver behaviour appropriate to the task or situation, despite this not being natural to them; to use the earlier metaphor, they pick the right spanner from the box.

I contend that effective management development, as well as encouraging people to play to their strengths, must also help individuals to feel confident to practise and deliver those behaviours that are less natural to them. However, nobody can be perfect all the time in how they behave and, therefore, reflecting on Lewin's 'equation', sometimes it is important to try to choose to operate in situations that allow greater application of one's Predispositions.

This is particularly pertinent to the selection and ongoing management of one's career occupation. Teams made up of diversely different Predisposition type individuals can often be highly effective, both at the collective as well as the individual level. **Great teams make great individuals more so than great individuals make great teams.**

At this point, it is worthwhile considering the character of the best teams that you have experienced. Were the participants similar or different in their character or nature? In thinking about this, consider the actual delivered behaviours that you observed and experienced.

Every Predisposition type has, by definition, a positive and negative aspect. Managers and leaders wanting to deliver superior performance need to understand their Predispositional make-up and consciously learn an array of alternative behaviours that they can deploy in the different situations they encounter.

It is vital to accept the key point that any one individual Predisposition profile will never satisfy the requirement of every situation.

The GPI™ Framework

Over the last twelve years, through research and practical application, the Glowinkowski Predisposition Indicator, or GPI™, has been devised to provide a highly statistically reliable indication of people's Predispositions.

The Predisposition framework consists of 19 bi-polar dimensions. In order to both present and position these dimensions in a more practical and organisationally relevant manner, the framework is structured in the context of three core factors of predisposition. This is depicted in Figure 5.1.

A High Level Model of an Individual's Predispositions

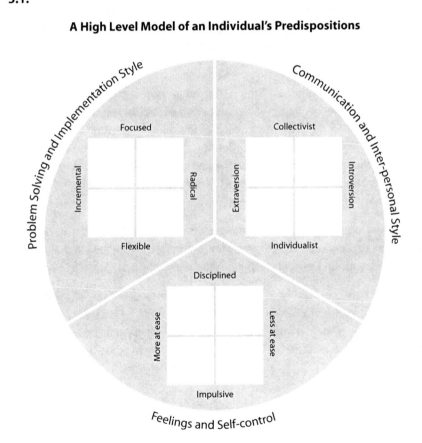

Figure 5.1

This model examines three Predispositional frameworks, namely:

- Problem Solving and Implementation

- Communication and Interpersonal Style

- Feelings and Self-control

The next section looks at these frameworks in detail and provides definitions of all the various components, which are summarised in the Appendices.

The stylistic representation of each core framework comprises two axes forming a four quadrant model. In Problem Solving and Implementation, an individual's preferred thinking style is 'married' to his preferred approach to doing tasks. In Communication and Inter-personal Style, an individual's preference to be with others or by himself is 'married' to his *teaminess*. In Feelings and Self-control, we marry the extent to which an individual feels okay about himself to the extent to which he controls his emotions.

Whereas in many instruments of this nature an axis will depict a linear scale, i.e. 0 to 100, which carries an interpretative risk of an individual regarding his score as being good or bad, the two axes in each of the three frameworks are 'bi-polar' in construction. This means the further out from the centre that an individual's data point rests, the more strongly held is that particular Predisposition. Therefore, the developmental 'effort' required to deliver the behaviour represented by the opposite side of the axis is much greater.

How willing an individual is to behave outside his predisposition is down to motivation, e.g. ambition to get on, and how comfortable he feels is down to the effort he expends on learning to operate differently.

As in the last chapter, I am now going to provide some detailed explanation of all the component dimensions and sub-scales of the GPI™. I encourage you to go through each explanation and consider where you sit on each scale and why you think this. GPI™ can be accessed by contacting info@glowinkowski.com.

Problem Solving and Implementation Style

In this framework, an individual's preferred style of thinking and preferred style of doing work activity is considered. In the two-by-two framework, the horizontal axis is labelled 'Incremental' and 'Radical', and the vertical axis is labelled 'Focused' and 'Flexible'; see Figure 5.2.

Problem Solving and Implementation Style

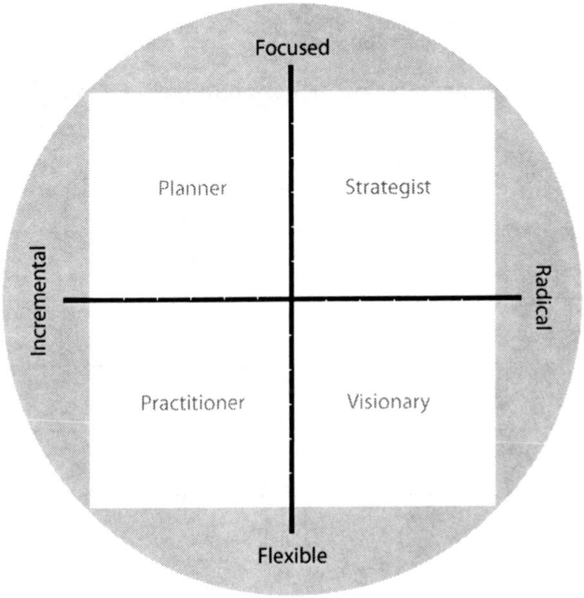

Figure 5.2

The Incremental-Radical dimension

This relates to the natural approach or style of thinking and decision-making that an individual prefers to bring to a particular situation or problem.

- ## The Incremental thinker

  This relates to an individual who prefers a more careful step-by-step approach to thinking about a particular situation, considering the more concrete and practical aspects of problem resolution and exercising a clear decision-making mechanism based on facts and information.

- ## The Radical thinker

Here the individual is predisposed to generate more creative ideas to a solution. He will have a propensity to prefer more abstract and conceptual problems and to be more interested in the longer-term type aspects of a problem. His decision-making is fundamentally based on intuition or gut-feeling rather than facts and figures.

Behind this primary dimension are three sub-scales which provide more detailed consideration of an individual's preferred thinking style; see Table 5.1.

Incremental	Radical
Evolutionary	Revolutionary
Practical	Conceptual
Rational	Intuitive

Table 5.1

Sub-scale: Evolutionary/Revolutionary

- An individual at the Evolutionary end of the scale will tend to approach a problem in terms of improvement, rather than more dramatic, seismic change. The natural, almost unconscious approach will be for the individual to think in terms of modification, evolution and improvement.

- At the other end of this dimension, we talk about a Revolutionary Predisposition. Here the individual is more likely to see a solution in much 'bigger change' terms. The individual's approach is likely to be more one of 'change': perhaps 'clean sheet of paper', rather than 'improvement'.

Sub-scale: Practical/Conceptual

- A Practical problem-solver is more orientated to consider specific tasks and tends to prefer to seek, assimilate and apply information relating to the problem and deliver practical solutions, which solve the immediate issue.

- The Conceptual problem solver is more comfortable acquiring, assimilating and applying information that is more abstract and relates to longer-term strategic and conceptual matters. He can easily link and associate disparate sources of information to position particular issues within a 'bigger picture'.

Sub-scale: Rational/Intuitive

- The Rational problem-solver will base his decision-making on facts and figures. These types prefer proof and clear definition about how to approach a particular problem.

- A more Intuitive thinker tends to have a preference for his own gut-feeling and instinct. He often feels, "I know this is the right way of doing things, just trust me".

The Focused-Flexible dimension

This relates to the natural approach or style that individuals prefer to take to carrying out task(s), i.e. how they like to do things.

- ## The Focused person

  A Focused person is an individual who enjoys structure and having a clear definition about what needs to be done; he enjoys the detail and operating to exacting standards of excellence.

• **The Flexible person**

A Flexible individual is far more 'loosely coupled' requiring less structure and definition; these people are more 'open-minded'. This includes the manner in which the organisation they work is assembled. They tend not to enjoy the detail and their approach will be more orientated towards being 'fit for purpose'.

Behind this main dimension are three sub-scales, which are listed in Table 5.2 and then explained in more detail below.

Focused	Flexible
Outcome	Spontaneous
Conscientious	Cursory
Perfectionist	Pragmatic

Table 5.2

Sub-scale: Outcome/Spontaneous

- An Outcome-orientated individual is considered to be a person who prefers a task or process of delivery that is well-defined in terms of its milestones, i.e. delivery date, specification, budget. Completion is at the forefront of his mind; he is orientated towards the destination rather than the journey. Being asked to do something extra may faze him as it disrupts his plans, i.e. he has gone into work that day to do A, B and C and won't be best pleased if asked to do D. An Outcome-orientated individual is likely to be seen as highly structured and 'well organised' in his approach; he keeps a tidy desk!

- The other end of the continuum is the Spontaneous style. Individuals with this style prefer to keep their options open and would be far less likely either to want or require - or, indeed, deliver - what we might describe as a detailed explanation of how something will happen and by when. They have a tendency not to commit to specific and defined outcomes or action steps and prefer what they would regard as a more *fluid* or *flexible* approach. They like to have lots of things running contemporaneously and are not fazed when asked to consider doing something else. Indeed, the interruption may be welcomed as it represents something new. They are less organised and, perhaps, work in a more cluttered environment.

Sub-scale: Conscientious/Cursory

- A Conscientious individual is someone who prefers to dot all the I's and cross all the T's. These individuals enjoy analysing the detail and need to know every aspect of a piece of work. They like to understand the detail of the delivery to be made. They will read the hefty report in full. They prefer to have time to prepare and rehearse presentations they are asked to make.

- A Cursory individual possesses less of a 'desire' or 'passion' for detail. He will tend to be more relaxed with a high level description of what he is being asked to do, i.e. guidance rather than instruction. He will read the Executive Summary rather than the whole report; he prefers brief bullet points rather than detailed documentation. His preference would be to leave the detail to someone else. He will feel comfortable making a presentation on the spur of the moment.

Sub-scale: Perfectionist/Pragmatist

- The Perfectionist strongly desires perfection in all that is around him: the Sale poster in the shop window has to be plumb vertical; there can be no spelling mistakes on his presentation slides; what he considers excellent today is less acceptable tomorrow; he wants to continuously improve the standards and quality of what he produces.

- The Pragmatist is much more oriented to the 80/20, 'fit-for-purpose' approach, orientated towards providing products, solutions and processes that 'seem to do the job'. He would think and say, "If it's not broken, don't change it".

Interpreting different Problem Solving and Implementation styles

Data provided from the GPI™ needs to be considered both at the level of the individual scales but, more critically, through considering various combinations of those scales.

The first consideration is by looking where ones 'score' sits on the primary two-by-two matrix. The two axes generate four quadrants which are labelled (starting bottom right and moving anti-clockwise):

- Visionary

- Strategist

- Planner

- Practitioner

The categories represent what we might describe as 'personality types'.

The Visionary (Radical and Flexible)

- Towards the more extreme levels of these two scores we might describe a Visionary as an individual who thoroughly enjoys the bigger picture and likes to keep a variety of activities at the forefront of his attention.

- As leaders, these people may like to inspire a creative work environment, where lots of ideas are generated; to many this appears to be the 'sexy' quadrant. However, a downside might be that the sheer flood of ideas may cloud any sense of clarity as attention switches from this week's 'great idea' to something different next week.

The Strategist (Radical and Focused)

- Similar to the Visionary, the Strategist prefers to think about the bigger picture, but will more deliberately consider implementation of his ideas than a Visionary.

- The Strategist's idea to, say, double profitability in five years is underpinned by consideration of what this means in terms of annual progress. He is likely to create 'target' business, organisational and operational models and could be a little 'precious' about these.

- He is likely to feel less comfortable dealing with the day-to-day minutiae of organisational life.

The Planner (Incremental and Focused)

- Planners are likely to be more at home with the idea of a specific and practical set of activities towards which they are able to make clear and steady progress to complete.

- They are more meticulous in planning what needs to be done and in what order. They will think more consciously about the contingencies and 'what ifs' in planning what has to be done, either sequentially or in parallel.

The Practitioner (Incremental and Flexible)

- The Practitioner simply likes to be immersed in doing 'lots of small stuff'. They prefer to make things better, e.g. repairs; note, however, **not** to the extent of making them perfect.

- They will juggle tasks, doing bits here and there in a more random, less structured manner.

These quadrants are useful but, nonetheless, are rather simplistic. While an individual may show an initial score, say, *north* of the axis on Focus/Flexible, they could have sub-scale scores *south* of the axis. For example, an individual who comes out as an overall Visionary might score Rational on the Rational/Intuitive sub-scale and Perfectionist on the Perfectionist/Pragmatic sub-scale. We might see most of the characteristics described as part of the Visionary type, but they tend to be more data- orientated in their decision-making, e.g. they may prefer to conjecture creative ideas out of a wide array of information and sources but suppress them in their own mind by virtue of not having 'proof positive'. Their Perfectionism may result in their expending intense effort at the eleventh hour to deliver something excellent when their Spontaneous, Cursoriness has not impelled them to think about delivery date and detail.

Such opposing factors can create natural in-built tensions which developing the means to 'act out of character' can help alleviate. This is helpful not just in terms of enhancing the likely performance delivered but also from a perspective of well-being.

Communication and Interpersonal Style

This second framework of the GPI™ considers how an individual prefers to engage with others. The horizontal dimension is labelled 'Extroversion' and 'Introversion'. The vertical dimension is labelled 'Collectivist' and 'Individualist'; see Figure 5.3.

Communication and Inter-personal Style

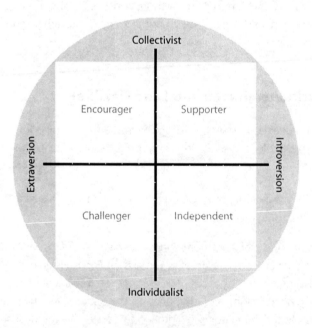

Figure 5.3

The Extroversion-Introversion dimension

It is important to note that I consider these two terms, like competency, to have been somewhat bruised by virtue of sight having been lost of their original tenor. This concerned how an individual energised themselves in the context of being with people or by themselves. The modern stereotypical image of the extrovert being the 'party-animal' is only part of the story.

- ## Extroversion

    The Extrovert is defined as an individual who is 'energised' by the opportunity for social engagement. Extroverts prefer to be in situations where they are able to interact with other people.

    Additionally, an individual predisposed to Extroversion is likely to be more comfortable articulating his views publicly and engaging and meeting with new people and acquaintances, together with possessing a fairly fun-loving demeanour.

- ## Introversion

    The Introvert is characterised as someone who generally prefers to focus on his own inner and private world; he enjoys his own company.

    Introverts tend to be more reflective, less likely to articulate their views in an assertive context, rather more serious-minded in their approach, with a tendency to be more selective in terms of social engagement.

The sub-scales for the Extroversion-Introversion dimension are presented in Table 5.3.

Extroversion	Introversion
Outgoing	Reserved
Assertive	Accepting
Fun Loving	Serious-minded
Self-assured	Uncertain

Table 5.3

Sub scale: Outgoing/Reserved

- An individual with an Outgoing predisposition is defined as having a preference to engage and interact with others. These types are energised through the company of others.

  They tend to learn through 'talking' and are motivated more by interaction than by individual reflection.

- The Reserved character is predisposed to the opposite of these tendencies. These character types tend to be more energised through their own company rather than by the company of others.

  They have a tendency to prefer to learn by 'thinking', rather than 'talking'. They are orientated to 'walk away' with a problem and think it through, rather than talk it over with others.

  As indicated, the key distinction is the idea of deriving energy as opposed to being fatigued. An Outgoing person is energised through the company of others, rather than wearied, whereas the Reserved character is far more energised through being in his own company.

  However, it must be added that we frequently see very reserved people who are highly skilled and perfectly comfortable in the company of others and, of course, vice versa. This is an ideal example lying at the heart of the differentiation between predisposition and delivered behaviour.

End of Day 1 on a two-day workshop

It can be interesting to see how these predispositional tendencies can manifest themselves in actual behaviours during workshops that we run.

At the end of the first day which has been spent in energetic discussion, when it is agreed to break for a while before dinner, those predisposed to be outgoing are quick to their feet asking colleagues to join them in the bar in order to continue the discussion. The more reserved types rise more slowly and sidle out of the room. When they come back downstairs for dinner, some remark they have lain on their beds for 30 minutes "enjoying the peace and quiet". They have re-charged their batteries ahead of an evening's further debate around the dining table.

Sub-scale: Assertive/Accepting

- Assertive individuals have a ready preference to articulate their views. At the extreme, they will be quite dominant when asserting these views.

  This contrasts with the more Accepting type where the individual has a tendency to 'keep his own counsel'. This is not to say that he doesn't assert himself, but he will only do so when he really has to, e.g. when his personal values are threatened.

Sub-scale: Fun-Loving/Serious Minded

- The more Fun-Loving in their approach will have a preference for activities in which they can enjoy themselves in the company of others; it is the element of Extroversion that matches the current stereotype. They seek pleasure in what they do; for instance, they may be more predisposed to watch the comedy channel on TV than a serious documentary. As managers, they want to create happy, enjoyable work environments.

  The Serious-Minded person, however, will tend towards more 'sober-minded' activities: rather than watch comedy, these individuals may elect to watch the History Channel or documentaries. They do not regard themselves as 'party-animals' and are generally less inclined to 'enjoy themselves in the company of others', than their Extrovert colleagues. In work, they are attuned to the duties, responsibilities and obligations of their role.

  We have seen some fascinating examples of apparently fun-loving individuals who, on one hand are regarded as the 'social secretary' of the work-group, including the Executive team, yet predispositionally are highly serious-minded. Their intent in arranging any social occasion for the team is to make it a great event, exceptionally well organised; they see that as a serious responsibility.

Sub-scale: Self-Assured/Socially Uncertain

- The Socially-Assured individual feels comfortable in all social contexts, including those involving meeting new people. These types are not especially socially selective in terms of only seeking out situations where they are likely to meet people they know. Such people are not fazed by mixing and engaging with large groups. When combined with the characteristic of Outgoing, such people are likely to be construed as possessing a highly 'socially engaging character'.

An individual who is Socially Uncertain is more selective and tends to find large groups and new company less enjoyable prospects. He is much more drawn to engaging with a more select group of colleagues, i.e. with people he knows. Socially Uncertain types often say that they find engaging in 'small talk' very difficult.

Again, we need to be careful not to confuse these predispositions with actual behaviour. Whatever predispositions are held, individuals can engage in delivering both their predispositions and the opposing behaviours.

I perform, I don't make presentations

Take the example of a Marketing Manager I know who is highly introverted across all sub-scales. Recognising this at University, she joined the drama society and is now able to play the character of a most engaging and gregarious individual. She 'performs' rather than makes presentations, and they are extremely impactful. However, she still enjoys long, solo walks in the countryside in order to have time on her own.

The Collectivist-Individualist dimension

This continuum considers what individuals seek to gain from their interactions with others.

The Collectivist

- Such people are often seen as warm, tender-minded and 'others' or 'people' orientated in their style. They talk more easily in terms of 'we' and are team orientated. They are approachable and seek the win-win, mutually beneficial outcome to their interactions.

The Individualist

- These individuals have a tendency to be more tough-minded and are seen as 'cold' rather than 'warm'. They are generally more 'self' rather than 'others' orientated. They talk in terms of 'I' and 'me'. They seek to gain more for themselves from an interaction than an evenly-balanced outcome, although this is not to suggest that they are duplicitous in their engagement style.

This overall dimension is also broken down in terms of four sub-scales which are shown in table 5.4 below.

Individualist	Collectivist
Unaffiliative	Affiliative
Questioning	Trusting
Dissenting	Conforming
Assuming	Modest

Table 5.4

Sub-scale: Affiliative/Unaffiliative

- An individual who has a predisposition for Affiliation is generally motivated to be seen as 'friendly' and 'warm'. He enjoys being liked by others and will enjoy being part of a social group for the opportunity to affiliate and engage with others.

- The Affiliative person may 'talk round' an issue, skirting direct mention of the matter for fear of causing upset, i.e. he will find giving critical feedback more difficult because he is worried about how the other person will react.

- An Unaffiliative individual is relatively less inclined to seek to act in a manner for which he will be liked. At the extreme, he could be seen as rather 'cold'.

These individuals will tend to find difficult 'people decisions' less problematic than will an Affiliative person. The down side is that an Unaffiliative person may simply 'wade in' and deliver feedback in an unduly blunt manner causing upset that clouds the intended message.

Sub-scale: Trusting/Questioning

- A Trusting person is likely to accept people at face value. A down side of the Trusting style is that the individual can make too many assumptions about other people; he can be easily hoodwinked or let down because he takes people at their word and, as a result, is often surprised later when things don't go as anticipated.

- An individual who is predisposed to be Questioning generally does not accept people at face-value. He tends to think about others' personal agendas and to have an orientation to be dubious or, at least, questioning about another person's motives and drivers. He will contemplate whether others have anything worthwhile to offer him. Perhaps at the extreme, these individuals can be sceptical or cynical.

Sub-scale: Conforming/Dissenting

- Conforming types tend to be seen as more 'agreeable' by their colleagues. Their predisposition is to conform rather than go against the prevailing norms of the group or organisation. At an unconscious level, conforming types tend to adopt a more 'group' or 'others' orientation in their decision-making, i.e. they put the group's interests before their own.

- A Dissenting individual has a predisposition to be less agreeable in terms of the group's view. At an unconscious level, he tends to generate his own thoughts, which are often quite different from the group's consensus.

  It is interesting to consider how this sub-scale marries with that of Assertive/Accepting.

- The Assertive/Dissenting type may be highly vocal in voicing his different view in meetings.

- The Accepting/Dissenting type could, however, sit there fulminating but unable to verbalise his different opinion, except afterwards in the corridor.

- The Assertive/Conforming type could be immensely positive towards the group's intent, perhaps being almost sycophantic towards the boss"s suggestion.

- The Accepting/Conforming type could sit there quietly nodding in agreement to the group's proposed activities.

This example shows how there is an infinite number of shades and colours to people's predispositions and that the relative scores on different sub-scales affect the potential impact that predispositions may have on delivered behaviour or the extent of the development journey to become proficient in delivering out of character behaviours.

Sub-scale: Assuming/Modest

- The Assuming type tends to see things more readily and clearly in terms of his own, rather than the group's contribution, e.g. "I did this". Modest types have a tendency to understate their role in activities; Assuming individuals could overstate their role in activities, which represents a down side for them because others could regard them as self-serving, possibly even pompous and arrogant. Modest types may also be more circumspect in providing praise. This is due to their not liking being put on a pedestal so they avoid putting others on one.

- An individual predisposed to be Modest is likely to be reluctant to talk about his achievements and accomplishments; these individuals don't readily 'blow their own trumpet'. They prefer to see outcomes and deliverables to which they have contributed as being the group's achievement more so than theirs, which provides an up side in that it will help generate a sense of inclusivity. However, this positive impact tends to be constrained by their not giving sufficient attention to how they will be perceived by others, i.e. they don't consider their 'personal brand' reputation.

Also, potentially, Modest types may be more circumspect about the veracity and validity of their views and opinions, whereas the Assuming individual is much more certain.

Interpreting different Communication and Inter-personal styles

As with the preceding framework, it is important to consider the inter-relationships between the different factors and or sub-scales; we have already considered this between Assertive/Accepting and Conforming/Dissenting. The two axes of the framework create four quadrants, labelled (starting bottom right and working around anti-clockwise):

- Independent

- Supporter

- Encourager

- Challenger

The Independent (Introvert and Individualistic)

- The Independent is likely to be perceived by others as somewhat cold and unwilling to engage voluntarily. However, when asked to contribute, he will do so and may take a contrary view to everyone else's. This is akin to the 12th man on the jury pronouncing a "not-guilty" verdict when eventually asked, despite the other 11 having said "guilty".*

The Supporter (Introvert and Collectivist)

- The Supporter shares the same introverted tendency as the Independent in terms of presenting others with difficulty in getting to know him. However, once this 'shell' has been cracked, these people are relatively warm and engaging and prefer to give counsel, guidance and advice rather than forceful views and opinions.

* One could use Henry Fonda's 1957 film Twelve Angry Men as an allegory, here.

The Encourager (Extrovert and Collectivist)

- Such individuals are often seen as warm and outgoing. They like to encourage and praise others but can find conflict and confrontation harder to address.

The Challenger (Extrovert and Individualist)

- They are likely to be perceived as highly engaging with others, but with a stronger, more tough-minded tendency. As managers, they strive to improve the extent and quality of their contribution to the organisation's goals, and expect likewise from their colleagues. Perhaps at the absolute extreme they could be harsh task masters, never satisfied and seeking to 'snatch all the glory' for themselves.

As before, looking at just the 'helicopter view' provided by the primary scale data being positioned somewhere within one of the four quadrants is helpful but provides a relatively simplistic view. Many individuals will have sub-scale scores that lie outside the quadrant.

For example, an individual who is Extrovert could be so by virtue of being strongly Outgoing and Fun-Loving, combined with more moderate Introvert aspects of Accepting and Social Uncertainty. Another could be Extrovert by virtue of being Assertive and Socially Assured, combined with Introvert aspects of Reserved and Serious-Minded. If these predisposition 'cocktails' are delivered as actual behaviour, two different styles would be witnessed, i.e. the more stereotypical extrovert compared to a more demonstrative and serious individual. Consider the former in a meeting that is getting slightly tense; does their predispositional tendency see them try to make some light-hearted remark, which may well ease the tension but could also be entirely the wrong input at that moment? The latter in a similarly tense situation may add to the tension by emphasising his view still more strongly. It could be the right behaviour to deliver; equally, it could be entirely wrong.

Similarly, too, with the Collectivist who could be Affiliative and Modest or Trusting and Conforming, which throw out potentially different behavioural tendencies.

Feelings and Self-control

The third framework generated by GPI™ considers how individuals regard themselves and how they control or govern their emotions and cravings; see Figure 5.4.

Feelings and Self-control

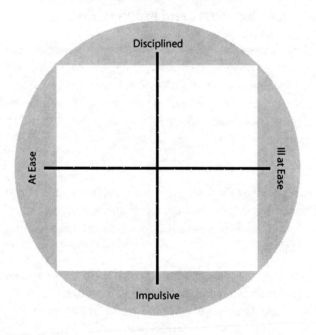

Figure 5.4

The Disciplined-Impulsive Dimension

- ### The Disciplined individual

  A Disciplined individual is someone who is generally predisposed to be quite low in the degree of openness in which they share their feelings and emotions with others. They also tend to be the types who control their immediate responses or urges in a particular situation. They have a tendency in behavioural terms to 'defer their response'.

They can remain cooler, calmer and more collected during pressured situations.

They know what is in the bank account and this caps their spending profligacy.

- ## The Impulsive type

  Such people tend to react in quite the opposite way to those predisposed to be Disciplined. They share more readily what they think with others; they wear their hearts on their sleeves – they are 'open books'.

  They will tend to make up their mind far more quickly and, rather than deferring a response to a particular situation or stimulus, will act quite rapidly; ask them something and the response is immediate.

  They go out and spend and only worry about money when the credit card bill arrives.

Overall, I consider this predispositional concept as underpinning Self-control.

The At Ease - Ill at Ease Dimension

While I have sought throughout GPI™ to step away from the pejorative sense of academic terminology, the fact that what is now being considered is how people rate themselves makes it impossible to create labels that do not infer some sense of criticism.

Unlike previously defined predispositions, this dimension can be seen as 'state' more than 'trait' in the sense that the current situation, especially if stressful, can influence the reported GPI™ profile in terms of being At Ease or Ill at Ease. Scores on these profiles can vary throughout a person's life, very much more so than in the previous dimensions that have been discussed.

- ## Being At Ease

  Such people feel good about themselves. They are not natural worriers; they consider themselves to be in a 'good place' in their lives; and they have a positive outlook and enjoy an air of self-confidence.

- ## Being Ill at Ease

  People Ill at Ease are more likely to worry; to fret about not having progressed as much as they would have liked in their lives; to perceive the future with a more jaundiced view; and to be harshly self-critical of their abilities.

The At Ease/Ill at Ease dimension includes four sub-scales, which are shown in table 5.5 below.

At Ease	Ill at Ease
Relaxed	Tense
Placid	Discontented
Optimistic	Pessimistic
Confident	Self-conscious

Table 5.5

Sub-scale: Relaxed/Tense

- This represents the extent to which an individual feels a sense of stress or strain in terms of their emotions. A Relaxed individual tends to feel far more laid-back, less worried, less keyed-up about particular situations, e.g. the outcome of a particular task.

- On the other hand, a Tense individual is less likely to be this way inclined and probably feels far more 'on-edge' and so tends to worry more about up and coming events. At the extreme, someone who is highly Tense could feel very anxious, whereas a more moderately Tense individual is more 'alert' to what is going on.

Sub-scale: Placid/Discontented

- An individual at the Placid end of this dimension is generally content and comfortable with his life, career and background; he is happy with his 'lot in life'.

- The concept of being Discontented relates to a person feeling a degree of regret about the past. At the extreme, an individual who is highly Discontented in terms of his profile is likely to feel quite angry and, perhaps, hostile towards situations and events from the past.

For some, being Discontented provides a positive 'fire in the belly' impelling them to do well; for some, it can be a much more corrosive aspect to their personality.

Sub-scale: Optimistic/Pessimistic

- An Optimistic person looks at the future in a positive way and is likely to regard the world fairly positively. Such people may be described as those who see the opportunities, i.e. 'the glass is half-full'.

- On the other hand, a Pessimistic individual has a tendency to see the world rather more negatively and might be described as 'always seeing the down-side' of a particular idea. He may be regarded as the sort of character who sees 'the glass half-empty'.

Sub-scale: Confident/Self-conscious

Overall, this sub-scale captures the idea of 'self-esteem'.

- If you wish, the Confident individual's conversation in the bathroom mirror in the morning is positive and upbeat, i.e. he values himself and is not overly concerned about his limitations. Potentially, at the extreme, this 'inner voice' is drowning out the genuine, supportive criticisms others are trying to make.

- The conversation of the Self-conscious individual is more critical and self-deprecating, talking himself down and highlighting his sense of limitation. At its 'loudest', the inner voice could be drowning out the genuine praise and plaudits that others are trying to pay to him.

That being Ill at Ease appears to present a more pejorative label oversimplifies the issue. We have worked with many examples of very high- performing people who come out as being Ill at Ease.   Furthermore, there are certain occupational groupings where we can observe a positive correlation between performance and being moderately Ill at Ease.

High-performing Air Traffic Controllers, Service Staff, Police and certain groups in the medical profession are often moderately tense, i.e. conveying a sense of being alert. Equally, whilst being Pessimistic can sometimes result in other people's ideas being 'fire-hosed', an Optimistic individual can miss important flaws in solutions by looking at the world through rose-tinted glasses. As a result, they have a habit of rushing into things, which turn out later to be somewhat of a 'bear-pit'. A Pessimistic tendency can sometimes be helpful in this regard by causing things to be considered more thoroughly. Pessimists are more risk-averse.

The key point with all of these factors is to think about how they relate and impact upon you in terms of your feelings about yourself. Do they affect your performance as a leader and general operator within your role?

It is helpful to use the GPI™ outputs to provide insight to the potential links with the competency areas discussed in Chapter 3. Given the right opportunity, complementary skills and knowledge of the individual, a natural flow from predisposition to behaviour can be expected. For example:

- In the context of the Problem-Solving and Implementation model, we would generally expect to see individuals in the Strategist and Visionary quadrants being far more comfortable in those areas of competencies relating to the bigger picture, so more adept at delivering behaviours such as Strategic and Conceptual Thinking and Customer Understanding. Additionally, we are likely to see a strong correlation with individuals in the Planner box in terms of behaviours such as Analytical and Forward Thinking, and Results Focus.

- Similarly we can look at the Communication and Inter-personal style framework.   Here, we are likely to see Outgoing and Affiliative individuals being much more likely to deliver effectively in terms of Relationship Building and Concern for Impact; but they may limit their

Independence behaviour because they want to curry popularity and avoid confrontational situations. Also, their Inter-personal Awareness may be less well honed because they are too busy talking instead of listening and watching.

In all of this, the need is to apply this thinking to yourself and to the teams you manage. What do you bring in with your personality? What is actually required? What do your teams bring, perhaps to 'close off' gaps in your own profile, so helping create a more rounded team capability?

Summary of Key Points

- Predispositions represent stable and relatively fixed characteristics of personality (except for At Ease and Ill at Ease, which is more state orientated).

- Predispositions represent what people are really like rather than their actual behaviour.

- If people behaved naturally then their predispositions would tend to be reflected through the behaviour they actually deliver.

- It is essential to interpret a GPI™ profile by considering the combination of dimensions, rather than just a series of independent 'measures'.

- Often predisposition is not reflected in delivered behaviour because:

  · There is no opportunity to deliver such behaviour.

  · The situation does not require it.

  · The situation does not allow it.

  · Insufficient skills and knowledge are possessed to fulfil it, i.e. it is almost impossible to assert something if you know nothing about it.

  · There is a lack of confidence.

- You will see people delivering behaviour that does not fit with their predispositions, because:

  · They have learned the uncharacteristic behaviour.

  · They are forced by circumstances to deliver the uncharacteristic behaviour, i.e. they have to cope with the situation.

  · Their behaviour is driven by a different predisposition, i.e. their need for power drives their acquisition of effective people engagement skills.

  · In certain situations, their values and beliefs drive their behaviour.

- Each predisposition has a positive and negative consequence given the circumstance, i.e. the task requirement. Therefore, one should avoid being negative about particular predispositions. Apart from specific situations or task requirements, there are no right or wrong profiles.

- From a team perspective it is good to have diversity in terms of individual profiles. Team members need to see the positive side of their colleagues' styles. If there are predisposition gaps in a team, the team members need to become aware of the potential weaknesses that they present for team performance.

  · Consider a team profile of all Visionaries, or all Planners. What are its inherent positive and negative attributes?

  · Consider a team profile of all Supporters, or all Challengers. What are its inherent positive and negative attributes?

Conclusion

The fundamental learning to take from this chapter is that analysing predispositions provides individuals with a deep insight into why they do what they do and why they feel uncomfortable when confronted by having to deliver certain types of behaviour.

The GPI™ commentary highlights individuals' natural behavioural strengths and illuminates their probable behavioural development needs which, if satisfied, will help them be more effective managers through exercising the necessary behaviours to build a high-performance Climate.

CHAPTER 6:

How Predisposition and Motivation influence actual behaviour

Over many years, my colleagues and I have provided feedback to thousands of people using the Glowinkowski Predisposition Indicator (GPI™) which I described in the previous chapter. The key objective of this work has been to help them to develop an understanding of:

- Why they do what they do

- Why they feel as they do

- Why it is that they tend to avoid certain types of activity

- What accounts for, or underpins, the style and type of behaviours they demonstrate.

For instance, does a particular activity seem to be more enjoyable, to be easier to do or, rather, is it a 'bit of a drag' and takes considerable and considered effort? Taken as a whole, an individual's Predisposition profile provides him with a powerful understanding of his more natural style of behaviour, which he is more likely to deliver or with which he feels more comfortable. In the context of these people being leaders and senior managers, they are able to appreciate more clearly why they may or may not deliver the types of behavioural competencies that we have discussed in the preceding chapters. For individuals, this 'data' is of great practical use because it helps them tailor their ongoing behavioural development and career progression. In other words, people can manage those potentially disruptive or dysfunctional (natural) behavioural inputs much more easily if they acquire a deep and comprehensive understanding of their causation and, concurrently, begin to practise those required behaviours which lie outside their comfort zone. On the positive side, knowing their natural strengths enables individuals to play to them.

In this sense, GPI™ feedback can be used practically, either from a personal development perspective, i.e. "What do I need to learn to be able to do?" or from a career management perspective in terms of seeking situations where an individual's natural strengths can be exercised. Within the situation of delivering feedback to a team, it enables members to appreciate each others' strengths and so help them operate in a manner where individuals can make distinctive contributions arising from those natural traits.

There are innumerable permutations of the GPI™ factors that were considered earlier and considerable effort is involved to understand them all. Through a series of specific one-to-one feedback sessions, individuals are helped to understand their 'predispositional' profile in terms of the practical implications it has towards their behaviour. It is extremely useful for people to establish this level of understanding, be they experienced leaders or, perhaps, youngsters about to embark on their work careers after completing their education.

In this chapter, I intend to go into more detail exploring how the various dimensions from the Predisposition frameworks link together and influence how individuals are likely to operate. I shall take a specific look at the type of linkage between the Predisposition sets and the types of competency behaviours discussed earlier. I shall do likewise with Motivation.

Predispositions

The *shape and colour* of a main dimension

As previously mentioned, each of the main GPI™ Frameworks has a series of facets, or sub-scales. While the aggregated score from these sub-scales locates a person's position on one of the main dimensions, it is essential to consider what we might describe as the 'shape' of sub-scales as this 'colours' the overall Predisposition dimension. Let us consider a few examples in order to provide you with some initial insights:

- ### The Extroversion and Introversion dimension

  Consider an individual who scores on the Extrovert side of the continuum. The immediate conclusion is that he will be an outgoing individual, which may well be the case. However, the underlying 'scores' on the component facets can suggest other characteristics.

  An individual who has responded to the questionnaire and is shown to be Reserved and highly Serious-Minded can quite readily demonstrate Introvert tendencies. If this individual is also reported to have a high score in Asserting and is Socially Assured, the overall score could well come out as Extrovert on the main dimension. See figure 6.1.

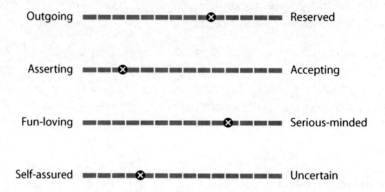

Figure 6.1

In this instance (if we assume that Predisposition results in actual, delivered behaviour), we are dealing with a style of Extroversion that is characterised by an individual who is confident in social situations involving people not known to him as well as feeling able to assert his views and opinions. However, the opposing scores indicate this individual to be less inclined to seek out social interaction and to prefer to devote himself to more serious subjects than those of levity. What may this mean?

It is likely that the individual will prefer to seek out only those social engagements that he considers relevant to his responsibilities and within which he could prove to be quite demonstrative. For instance, in a meeting, he may argue a particular point quite strongly.

On the other hand, if these scores are reversed, i.e. as depicted in Figure 6.2, the *locus* of the Extroversion is very different from that depicted in the previous illustration. It is more Outgoing and Fun-Loving.

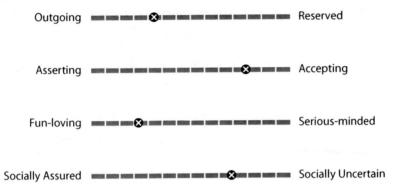

Figure 6.2

In this respect, while they may like 'mixing', it is more likely to be with those already known to them and that any contentiousness in a meeting is dealt with through humour.

(By the way, how the suggested styles of input to a meeting, i.e. demonstrative or jovial, are 'received' depends upon the context and, of course, the behaviours of the other participants which, in turn, may or may not reflect their Predispositions!)

Feelings and Self-control

Consider, for example, an Expressive individual characterised by being Tense and Impulsive, which would be rather different from an individual who is predispositionally Discontented, Pessimistic and Self-conscious.

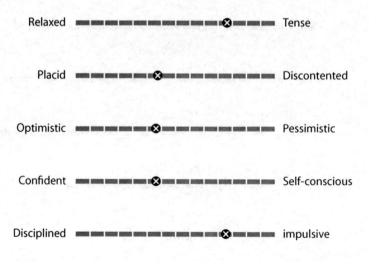

Figure 6.3

The suggestion conveyed by the profile in Figure 6.3 is that of a 'lively' individual who is likely to be keen to deliver a good job by virtue of naturally 'worrying' about what could go awry. He will be alert to issues and keen to address the detail in order to avoid making mistakes. Where these arise, a more volatile reaction may result.

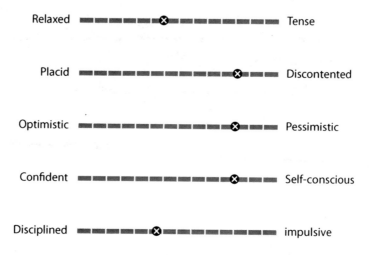

Figure 6.4

The profile in Figure 6.4 indicates an individual who is characterised by having deep levels of self-doubt, perhaps demonstrating a 'chip on the shoulder' type of behaviour with others (consider Eeyore in A.A. Milne's *Winnie the Pooh*[40]). Clearly, again, the profiles within the overall dimension that result from different 'blends' of the sub-scales are quite different.

The Radical and Incremental dimension

Consider someone who is Radical at the level of the main dimension but who is actually characterised at the facet level by being Revolutionary, Conceptual and Rational; see Figure 6.5.

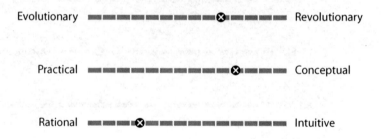

Figure 6.5

This individual prefers to 'think big', drawing upon data and information sourced from a broad swathe of origins that he weaves together to establish creative solutions to the challenges and problems he confronts. However, his Rationality possibly causes him to dismiss some ideas because he cannot 'prove' them logically in his own mind. However, someone who is also Intuitive rather than Rational may give 'flight' to more of his ideas because they 'feel right'. Someone who is the polar opposite may consider such thoughts to be, literally, 'flights of fancy'.

For the Incrementalist who is Evolutionary, Practical and Rational, his preferred approach to problem-solving is likely to be very thoroughly thought through, including some practical, experimental testing to provide empirical evidence, and then to re-think it through and test again.

For the Incrementalist who is more Intuitive than Rational, see Figure 6.6, he may well want to try out a few things that *feel* workable and see what happens; metaphorically, he thinks it may be worthwhile 'turning the nut another quarter turn'.

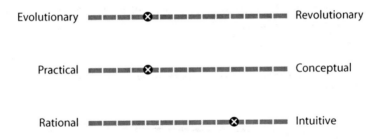

Figure 6.6

- ## The Individualist and Collectivist dimension

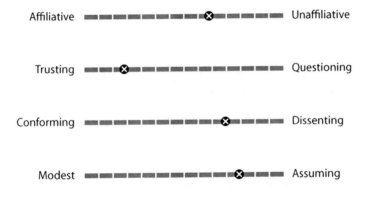

Figure 6.7

In the first instance, let us consider an Individualist who is Unaffiliative, Dissenting and Assuming, but is also highly Trusting, see Figure 6.7.

This type of character often delivers a relatively detached and cool behaviour yet, at the same time, exhibits a certain *naivety* in his response that draws in people, which some find touching. "They're sweeties, really," is a phrase that is sometimes used to describe such individuals.

However, with the exact opposite, i.e. a Collectivist who is Affiliative, Conforming and Modest, but demonstrates a high level of Questioning behaviour, see Figure 6.8.

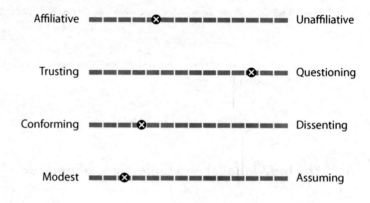

Affiliative ━━━━━⊗━━━━━━━━━━ Unaffiliative

Trusting ━━━━━━━━━━━⊗━━ Questioning

Conforming ━━━⊗━━━━━━━━━━ Dissenting

Modest ━━⊗━━━━━━━━━━ Assuming

Figure 6.8

This 'mix' of Predispositions may result in behaviour that is apparently warm, friendly and co-operative, but is made superficial by dint of the individual's inherent 'suspicion' towards others, which can cause others to wonder, "Where is [the individual] coming from?".

• ## The Focused and Flexible dimension

Further possibilities are generated by the various possible 'blends' created by this dimension. Focused individuals who are Outcome minded and Conscientious as well as Pragmatic are difficult to read in terms of what is driving them; see Figure 6.9.

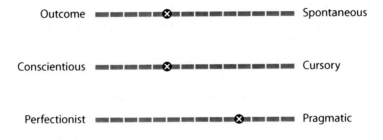

Figure 6.9

Their conscientious approach to achieving a particular goal can be construed as perfectionism until such time that a 'corner is cut' in order to get something completed. It is as if their effort is 'front-loaded' in terms of taking time to work out the plan of what to do and how, but then the delivery deadline creeps up on them and their Pragmatism gets them 'over the line'. Sometimes things work; at other times there are undue consequences, e.g. a system upgrade fails unexpectedly because 'User Acceptance Testing' was cut short.

Conversely, if we take a highly Flexible individual who is Spontaneous and Cursory in his style, yet concurrently demonstrates Perfectionism very strongly, see Figure 6.10.

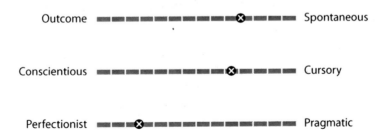

Figure 6.10

This person may well 'amble towards' doing something but, at the last moment in order to deliver something really good, he 'burns the midnight oil'. In this instance, the intent of his perfectionism is less concerned with absolute detail and accuracy but is much more about achievement. Such people may be motivated by 'kicking around' an intellectual concept, which eventually results in a perfected, detailed argument.

Tying the dimensions together

Within each of these short interpretive discussions, I have considered the 'shape and colour' of each dimension in a one-dimensional manner, i.e. within itself. This is only part of the debate. There is also the very vital need to combine dimensions from different frameworks, e.g. Radical and Incremental with Collectivist and Individualist, and between sub-scales, e.g. Assertive and Accepting with Disciplined and Impulsive.

It is helpful to try to 'picture' a three-dimensional combination, e.g. Radical and Incremental, with the two dimensions in the Communication and Inter-Personal Style framework. How will the different permutations present their ideas and what will they want from such interactions?

Thus, although an initial feedback session may well result in discussion on a 'point-by-point' basis, it is the subsequent reflection and follow-up sessions that provide really deep awareness for the individual of his preferred or natural behaviours, far more so than any other instrument of which I am aware.

From this sound knowledge base with subsequent support, individuals can map out the behavioural development needs that will see them acquire the ability to deliver, consciously and comfortably, a much broader array of behaviours into the different situations they encounter. They have, so to speak, more 'behavioural clubs' with which to play their managerial game.

For each dimension, I have considered only two of the possible permutations.

The key point in any GPI™ feedback process is to consider how the various aspects of this 'tapestry' actually fit together.

Links to the competencies

I have made the point that the link between Predisposition and actual behaviour can be quite tenuous. For a variety of reasons, people's behaviour, i.e. what they actually do, does not always reflect their 'natural' or 'preferred' style. We often do what is required by others or prevailing circumstances. Nowhere is this more the case than in the workplace, where the environment, lack of requisite knowledge, or limited interest blocks individuals acting as they would like. Despite this, however, we do observe correlation between predisposition and actual behaviour.

In this section, I will explain some of the connections between aspects of predisposition and the delivery of competencies and the higher order of behavioural approaches described within the Integrated Framework.

Problem-solving and implementation style

Incremental

The Incremental aspect of problem-solving and decision-making has its strongest relationships with the following competencies:

- Analytical Thinking

- Forward Thinking (at least in terms of planning more immediate rather than longer-term activities)

- Concern for Excellence

- (and, perhaps, certain aspects of) Results Focus.

In terms of their leadership 'approach' as defined by the higher order behaviours considered within the Integrated Framework, the most significant and noticeable relationship is seen in managers' leadership being more analytical and task-orientated. I expect to see Incrementalists deliver relatively poor effectiveness in Positional behaviour, which detracts from building up Autonomy within Climate. They find it difficult to 'let go of the nitty-gritty', preferring to do their team members' jobs more so than their own. They are reluctant to delegate. They may 'sit' on their people's shoulders, constantly checking and interfering.

Radical

The Radical aspect of problem-solving and decision-making is more congruent with the strategic side of the Thinking cluster within the competency framework. I would expect to see relatively strong associations with:

- Conceptual Thinking

- Strategic Thinking (although this doesn't necessarily follow because the individual may not have had any manifest opportunity to translate his broad conceptual thinking into the commercial and organisational context that hallmarks Strategic Thinking)

- Customer Understanding

- Forward Thinking, i.e. over a longer time-frame than the Incrementalist.

Additionally, a link to Strategic Influencing may also be seen because the individual's wide array of ideas is likely to form the basis of their change agenda which is, of course, the cornerstone of this behaviour.

Within the context of the Integrated Framework's leadership behaviours, I discern congruence with Directional behaviour. In short, Radical people are more predisposed to think about and, therefore, potentially communicate their perspectives of what the organisation's long-term direction should be. However, the effectiveness of their communication is also likely to be influenced by their Communication and Inter-personal styles. This, of course, links clearly to the formation of Clarity within Climate.

Flexible

The Flexible end of the Focused/Flexible continuum scores a number of distinctive hits against competency behaviour. I expect a highly Flexible person to demonstrate:

- Flexibility

- Conceptual Thinking

- Strategic Thinking

There may also be a degree of relationship with the Influencing behaviour of Inter-Personal Awareness because these people are likely to 'sense' what others want. However, if they try to accommodate everyone, this would cause counter-productive Concern for Impact to be demonstrated because, in essence, they are trying to please everyone - which tends to result in succeeding in pleasing no-one!

Additionally, I expect a connection between being Flexible by predisposition and Critical Information Seeking behaviour from the Achievement cluster. At first-hand, this may appear counter-intuitive. The basis of this is that the higher level of Critical Information Seeking behaviour requires an individual to take a broad perspective and keep an open mind to a wide range of variables.

Finally, there may also be some degree of correlation with the higher level of Concern for Excellence, where an open mind equips the Flexible individual with a natural inquisitiveness to look at other organisations, i.e. to 'benchmark'.

Focused

The Focused end of the continuum conveys a number of key delivered behavioural predictions. The most obvious, of course, is that with Results Focus because the predisposition entirely concerns an individual achieving a targeted outcome in an organised and prioritised manner. Note, however, that the link is likely to be with the more detailed delivery of this behaviour, i.e. his endeavours rather than those of others through delegation. In addition, a Focused individual is likely to deliver high levels of:

- Tenacity (because he is driven to achieve an outcome and, therefore, is less likely to be put off)

- Concern for Excellence (but at the tactical level rather than the broad scanning conducted by the Flexible).

Within the context of the Integrated Framework's Leadership Behaviours, I expect a Focused individual to be more prepared to deliver the Alignment aspect of Directional behaviour than Strategic or Long-Term Direction, i.e. he may not establish the initial vision or underlying idea of organisational intent but he is adept at then determining how to acquire and marshal the required resources to achieve the stated goal.

For this very reason, I have seen many successful 'partnerships' between a Flexible CEO and a Focused COO, FD or MD.

Communication and interpersonal style

Extroversion

Extroversion is likely to have a significant link with various aspects of Influencing. An Extrovert would be expected to deliver high levels of:

- Relationship Building (more likely to seek a higher frequency of interaction with other people)

- Concern for Impact

- Independence (especially in relation to an Extrovert who is highly Assertive)

For the Extrovert operating among a group of Introverts, he may deliver ineffective Concern for Impact simply by being too 'loud'; his effusiveness overwhelms others and builds resistance. A case in point concerned a new School Head trying to turn round results in a poorly performing school whose Governing Body and senior staff were less inclined to apply modern managerial practices. An *impasse* was reached until each understood through his own Predispositions where the others were coming from.

Within the higher order behaviours of the Integrated Framework, the Extrovert could be considered Engaging by virtue of his 'force of personality'. However, if this individual is leading a group of Introverts, he may not be regarded as either Engaging or Constructive but, instead, as superficial due to the manner in which he relates to others and the quality of the relationships he tries to cultivate.

Introversion

The Introvert will have a very different style of Influence compared to the Extrovert. It is often the case that Introverted individuals tend to deliver higher levels of Inter-personal Awareness by virtue of being quieter; they watch and listen more. (Talking and listening concurrently is a virtual impossibility.)

It may also be the case that the Introvert delivers a higher level of ability in Strategic Influencing because his more reflective approach renders a more measured engagement style over the longer term. As such, his Relationship Building, although not 'easy', could be construed as being orientated more towards *mutual benefit* than is probably conveyed by the Extrovert. This is especially the case where the other person is predispositionally Questioning and may, therefore, 'smell a rat', i.e. be suspicious of the Extrovert's ulterior motives.

Introversion also impacts aspects of Thinking since it is likely that an Introvert will tend to deliver a more reflective type of thinking which may, therefore, result in a greater degree of Conceptual Thinking and Strategic Thinking.

Collectivist

Collectivism will have significant links with various aspects of Influencing. Relatively strong connections are likely to be seen with:

- Inter-personal Awareness

- Concern for Impact

These behaviours are delivered in the guise of being somewhat affiliative and 'people pleasing' rather than assertive and challenging. Within this, of course, there is a clear negative relationship between Collectivism and Independence because such people are driven to please and, therefore, they are unlikely to speak their mind or raise difficult issues because conflict may ensue.

Furthermore, there is an interesting relationship between being Collectivist and the behaviour of Developing Others. On the one hand, the individual will be clearly motivated to help individual colleagues. However, real 'help' in development terms necessitates confronting poor performance, which the Collectivist is less likely to do. As a result, poor performance may be tolerated by virtue of lack of inclination - or, more seriously, inability - to address the underlying issue. Any coaching that does occur is benign and, realistically, is no more than a pat on the back which, while merited, may be more beneficial if it is construed by the recipient as meaning, 'More, please!'

This presents a clear link with the Development behavioural approach within the Integrated Framework. Furthermore, the Collectivist is likely to seek to build relationships although may be less likely to deal with friction as it arises. Their delivery of the Constructive behavioural approach from the Integrated Framework could be 'mixed'. Similarly, the Collectivist could be highly Democratic by looking to include and involve everyone in determining what is to be done. 'Planning by committee', in my experience, is not necessarily an effective approach.

Individualist

An Individualist will tend to show opposite connections than those described above. I would expect to see negative correlations within Inter-personal Awareness and Concern for Impact, since the main preoccupation of the Individualist is himself. However, one needs to take care here because the Individualist may be motivated to influence others for manipulative reasons to get something done for his own benefit. Thus, while he may appear to be paying attention and engaging with subtle impact, he is not actually attempting to ingratiate himself with others but, instead, is making something happen for his own gain. Such behaviour can 'work' in the short term but, for those whose own Inter-personal Awareness is more keenly attuned, they may spot the duplicity and divisiveness and, possibly, react to the Machiavellian style of influencing* and 41.

The Individualist poses an interesting relationship with Developing Others since, unlike the Collectivist, the Individualist will have no difficulty in surfacing difficult issues with others and generating a degree of conflict. The question is whether the resultant tension is healthy or destructive, i.e. is it truly developmental or does it simply result in others 'kow-towing' in order to avoid further criticism? Wherever and whenever the Individualist delivers constructive feedback and the degree of *directional* coaching required to raise performance, it is more than likely that he is also exercising Independence and Concern for Impact, i.e. speaking his mind about others' performance but in a manner that is less likely to be construed as unwarranted criticism.

The Individualist could exercise sound Positional behaviour within the construct of the Integrated Framework. He will do his job. However, in being concerned about his own image, he could interfere with what others do if he is concerned about any possible negative ramification for how he perceives that he is regarded. The Individualist is more likely to address issues within relationships, i.e. to manage conflict within the Constructive leadership behaviour approach. However, the Individualist may not be especially Democratic and could create some organisational schisms by only involving people he thinks will go along with his view of things.

---

* Niccolo Machiavelli was a famous politician in Florence, Italy in the 16th century. He has become synonymous with 'success by any means', displacing traditional moral values for ruthlessness, deception and, in some cases, outright cruelty. Machiavellianism is regarded as one of three traits that are part of the 'Dark Triad' of personality, the others being psychopathy and narcissism. It concerns being 'in it for oneself' rather than for the team.

Feelings and Self-Control

At Ease and Ill at Ease

The links and associations between the predispositional states (remember I remarked earlier that these Predispositions are more *state*, i.e. affected by the circumstance of the moment, than fixed *traits* of personality) and delivered behaviours are more nebulous and quixotic. They do need to be considered carefully against the individual's situation and circumstance. However, let me offer a few initial observations to help your own thinking.

The individual who is At Ease with himself may feel more confident and comfortable thinking more broadly and longer into the future than the Ill at Ease person, who may be more inclined to worry about the 'here and now' and so think more deeply and in detail about matters, i.e. Conceptual and Strategic from the former; Analytical and contingency component of Forward Thinking from the latter.

The At Ease individual may feel more comfortable engaging with others and influencing them, but others may construe him to be overly confident, perhaps even arrogant. The Ill at Ease may come across as lacking the necessary 'punch' to win the argument and discussion.

The At Ease person may lack the inclination to polish his final delivery, feeling that his effort is good enough, so resulting in limited Concern for Excellence. His intent to dig into things may also be self-limiting, constraining his Critical Information Seeking. The Ill at Ease may fret too much about the 'quality' of his output and worry about having missed something, that he may deliver too much tactical Concern for Excellence and persistently check for more information. He may miss delivery deadlines due to these worries.

The At Ease individual is more likely to have the confidence to exercise Independence than the Ill at Ease. An interesting correlation we have seen is that the At Ease may be less Flexible and oriented to Self-Development, i.e. an arrogance of view about his having a need to take on board others' points of view or to learn.

Disciplined and Impulsive

An essential correlation for the Disciplined individual is in Tenacity; he has the natural ability to concentrate over long periods of time and not have his attention diverted by other things. The Impulsive can get bored quickly and be easily distracted. This has interesting outcomes across the full gamut of other competency clusters, i.e.

thinking, influencing and achieving – there are fleeting bursts of behaviour related to something then something else 'catches the mind'.

The connections here are less 'fixed' and there is little point trying to consider all the nuances and quirks. However, we encourage you to think of other possible links in respect of your own Predispositional tendencies and behaviours and for those of the people with whom you work.

The associations between these different predispositional states and the quality of delivering the higher order behaviours of the Integrated Framework is both complex and likely to be in a constant state of flux. It is absolutely a case of considering each individual individually.

Motivation

I want now to give some further thought to Motivation, over and above that which occurred in the opening chapter of the book. Motivation represents another aspect of an individual's set of characteristics. In Chapter 1, I mentioned Maslow and Herzberg.

The Integrated Framework (see below, Figure 6.12) clearly illustrates that the leader's critical role is the creation of a high-performance Climate. It is his motivations that stimulate him to do this. He is not, as I commented during Chapter 3, motivating other people. This is what Herzberg recognised in his work.

The Glowinkowski Integrated Framework

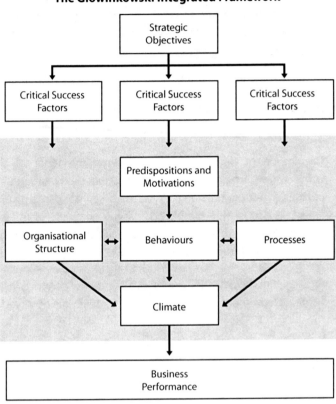

Figure 6.11

The mantra of "he who shouts loudest longest", to which Herzberg attached the more colourful epithet of the 'kick in the ass' approach (KITA), simply does not work. Command and control does not produce a sustainable high- performance Climate. Even when the building is on fire, shouting and bellowing "Get out!" is more likely to induce panic. Perhaps Dwight D. Eisenhower, a US President, summed it up best of all, when remarking, "You do not lead by hitting people over the head – that's assault, not leadership."[42]

In my study of motivation, I wanted to consider the influence of motivations upon behaviour from a number of angles. Firstly, I wanted to address the concept from the perspective of the social motives that were first put forward by Charles Murray (1938)[43] and David McClelland (1985). McClelland defined a framework of social motives, the idea being that individuals were driven by one or more of three internal motivational drivers, which included Need for Achievement, Need for Affiliation and Need for Power. Secondly, I wanted to consider matters from the stance of more recent research conducted by colleagues, which deliberately took a narrower focus into the field of leadership and management.

It is still appropriate to consider the link between the social motives and behaviour.

The impact of 'need for Achievement' upon behavioural delivery

- The important distinction here concerns the tenor of the word 'achievement', which concerns an individual being strongly driven to personally out-perform against his own set standards of excellence. Thus, it is deeper than simply achieving a goal, i.e. it is not just about winning the race, so to speak, but it is doing so in a faster time than that previously run by the individual.

  As a result of the definition adopted, a number of connections between strong achievement motivation and competency are observed, e.g.:

  o Results Focus

  o Concern for Excellence

  o Initiative

  o Analytical Thinking

  o Independence

  o Tenacity

  In general terms, people high in achievement motivation tend to be highly task-focused, which tends to dilute Influencing competencies.

  In the context of the Integrated Framework, high achievement motivation can cause a low-level of delegation and achieving through other's endeavours, i.e. poor Positional behaviour. Such people want to do it all themselves because no-one else can do it as well they can.

All this presents a fascinating organisational conundrum; a real paradox. Achievement motivation is the motive of the individual contributor; someone who delivers. This is often the very characteristic that sees people get promoted (to quite senior positions, too). Yet, once promoted, this overarching desire to do everything for themselves becomes problematic and counter-productive to being an effective leader or manager. Practically, consider an excellent sales person or engineer who is promoted to run the team but proves to be ineffective. Perhaps such situations lie behind the caustic comment of, "He was promoted to the limit of her/his incompetence"?

In such situations, much of our feedback concentrates upon identifying the ways and means by which individuals can manage their high achievement motivation and learn to let go and delegate effectively.

The impact of 'need for Affiliation' upon behavioural delivery

- Put simply, this motivational need concerns enjoying being liked. In a more complete sense, individuals thus motivated want to maintain the quality and harmony in a relationship. As a result, I expect to see strong links with:

o Relationship Building

o Inter-personal Awareness

o Concern for Impact

Individuals want to form relationships with others and curry favour by engaging with them in a manner that will not cause offence or upset but will, rather, please. Accordingly, one would expect the individual to 'charm' others; at the more extreme, the behaviour could be ingratiating, obsequious, possibly sycophantic.

For individuals high in affiliation, they are less likely to deliver Independence behaviour because 'saying their piece' and raising difficult issues will cause discord in any relationship, which they do not want. Also, certain aspects of Results Focus and Tenacity may be lacking because their need to please others will tend to constrain their driving other people to complete and deliver set tasks and objectives. Yet things are not so straightforward because someone who works hard to be liked may well be liked, which results in others striving to do more for him without being directed.

"Attention!"

In one piece of work with a senior manager who was highly affiliative and had previously been a reasonably high-ranking officer in the army, he was almost avuncular to his immediate reports in ensuring they were looked after. This affiliative motive did not manifest itself, however, in behavioural terms when he dealt with other departments, e.g. Logistics, where his bite was considered far worse than his bark.

Why? His short temper and acute impatience was exercised by virtue of wanting to get everything his team needed to do its dangerous job. He was charm personified to them but immensely demanding towards everyone else. Without doubt, his men would do his bidding; they would, and indeed did, 'go over the top for him.'*

The impact of need for Power

- Principally, Power relates to the idea of the individual being driven by a strong need to influence, impact and control others and enjoying doing so.

    McClelland distinguished between the two 'faces' of Power, namely *personalised* and *socialised* power.

    o Personalised power

    This is about enjoying the trappings of power, the status, the position, the opportunity to give orders. It lies at the root of the accusations concerning senior leaders and managers 'feathering their own nests' before considering anyone else.

    o Socialised power

---

* It is important to consider the adverse consequence of this in that I have also seen this go too far, e.g. the manager who gets his team to 'break the rules' in order to achieve goals. At the time of writing, such coercion is suggested as a causal factor to the banking crisis.

This concerns the leader or manager who endeavours to create an environment, or Climate, that *feels* good to be in. It is not about creating something cosy or overtly comfortable but, rather, an organisational setting where there is a sense of collaborative ambition and mutual objectivity, i.e. a 'one for all, and all for one' style of approach.[44]

In all our work, personalised power **never** delivers the same degree of positive outcomes as socialised power. Even in the most dramatic of turn-round or crisis situations, draconian application of personalised power is more likely to make matters worse.

Therefore, I expect to see (socialised) Power motivation connected to a range of Influencing behaviours, particularly:

o Relationship Building

o Strategic Influencing

o Concern for Impact

o Inter-personal Awareness

These stem from individuals wanting to establish a body of people they can influence and control to bring about the realisation of their plan, or their 'vision'. Inter-personal Awareness is especially important because by recognising others' 'hot buttons', when these are pressed through adept adjustment of their Concern for Impact behaviour, they are more likely to be won over to the individual's point of view.

Additionally, also expected to be seen is a strong association with Strategic Thinking because individuals motivated by Power will, as intimated in the previous paragraph, have their own vision for how things can be done differently and better. This forms the fulcrum on which they seek to influence others. Thereafter, it is highly likely that Development of Others competency will be strong because achieving their vision is dependent upon others doing things for them. They recognise their own limitations in not being able to do everything themselves and look to acquire people who can complete all these other necessary activities. In order that these are done proficiently, the individual feels compelled to train and develop others.

As with Predispositions, there are different 'mixes' of motivation that will result in different behavioural outcomes. For instance, the likely *flavour* of behaviour from an individual with high achievement, low affiliation and high power will be entirely different from that of an individual with low achievement, high affiliation and high power. The former may be more the single-minded entrepreneur or specialist who finds it hard to let go and delegate to new employees in their growing enterprise. The latter may like being the boss but is far too tolerant of poor performance. In both situations, these leaders could steer their organisations down a slippery slope to failure.

A more modern interpretation of Motivation in a managerial context

In my research and consultancy experience with my colleagues, it had become increasingly clear that while McClelland (and, previously, Murray) answered certain questions concerning managers' effectiveness in creating a high-performance Climate, it didn't 'dig deep enough'. Something seemed to be missing. Several years ago, therefore, I initiated an intensive research programme in order to establish a more comprehensive framework with respect to individual motivation.

This resulted (through statistical analysis techniques, e.g. factor analysis) in identifying six principal factors of motivation, which cover both extrinsic and intrinsic aspects. These six factors are:

* **Power**

  This concerns the extent to which an individual is motivated to have influence and control over the actions, thoughts and behaviour of others. This can be simply limited to absolute authority and control, which is termed Personalised Power, i.e. power for power's sake, or extended to include the power achieved by influencing others for the greater good of what is trying to be achieved, termed Social Power.

* **Relationships**

  This concerns the development of deep and significant relationships with others. It is where relationships are considered to be truly motivational in themselves rather than simply being needed in order to deliver a particular outcome. This dimension recognises individuals who are highly motivated to avoid circumstances that may disrupt the harmony of the relationship to the extent that it can be regarded as a strong desire to be liked or approved.

• Achievement

This is about the extent to which an individual is motivated by his own activities and efforts, which result in successful outcomes. We are not considering more general achievements, i.e. those delivered by the team or group of which the individual is a member; we are focusing distinctly on the individual's own contributions, relating to how he has responded to challenges and managed his own growth and development. This factor also considers ambition, in the sense that striving and achieving ambition goals is, in itself, motivational.

• Status

This is the extent to which an individual is driven to attain a 'position in life', evidenced by tangible measures of success which encompass the visible signs that the person has 'done well'. Demonstrating this success is important to such an individual. Social status is also important as this reflects an individual's position within the organisation or community.

• Recognition

This reflects the extent to which an individual is driven by a need to be recognised and appreciated by others i.e. those respected by the individual. An individual attaches importance to perceiving that 'significant' others (close friends and colleagues) value and respect him. This differs from Relationships, as Recognition is about value and respect as opposed to being liked. It also includes being valued by a wider range of people, so being recognised in the broader social network.

- ### Esteem

  This concerns the need to be encouraged through acquiring positive feedback. Praise, which confirms to an individual that he has performed well, can also serve to overcome any potential fear of failure. For some, avoiding failure can be a big motivator.

Within each of the six groups lie a number of more detailed elements, which are listed in table 6.1. These provide the means, as indicated when defining power earlier, to determine the extent of personalised or socialised power held by an individual and the degree to which extrinsic motivation is considered important.

Power	Relationships	Achievement
Influence Control Authoritative	Friendship Affection Approval Colleagueship	Challenge Excellence Growth Ambition
Status	**Recognition**	**Esteem**
Pay Wealth Accumulation Social Status	Respect Valued Reputation	Fear of Failure Feedback

Table 6.1

The data arising from an individual completing the Glowinkowski Motivational Indicator questionnaire is presented in a number of formats. An example is provided in Figure 6.12

Hierarchy of Motives

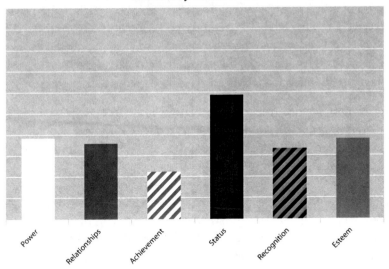

Hierarchy of Motives

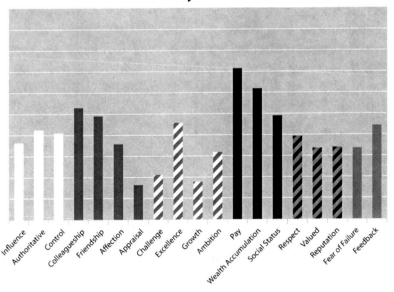

Figure 6.12

Through its style of questioning, it is worth noting that our new measure of motivation provides two assessments for the individual (a third output considers preferred styles of work, commented upon by writers such as Chris Argyris and Donald Schön[45]). The first set of questions is structured in a traditional style of single items requiring the respondent to 'score' them on a one-to-five scale (for the technically minded, a Likert scale: Rensis Likert devised this technique of responding to questionnaires during the 1930s[46]). The output from these questions provides an overview of the level of importance the individual attaches to the different groups of motivation.

The second set of questions presents the respondent with groups of three statements from which the respondent has to say which is 'most' like him and which is 'least' like him. (This style of questioning is called *ipsative*, or 'forced choice'.) Here, having asked the first set of questions, we are now asking the individual to make some choices, i.e. to rank the motivations in levels of importance. The resultant data is highly informative in helping individuals understand if their current role is truly motivating for them or, alternatively, whether any new role they are considering as their next career move will motivate them. It provides a kind of personal/internal hierarchy of motivational drivers.

If what they identify as most important is not being provided by their existing role, their likely performance contribution is going to be lower than it could be. It is important that their manager engages with them in some meaningfully detailed conversation about what they want. A critical responsibility of management and leadership is to ensure that the organisation comprises people who want to be there. Helping someone leave to get into somewhere they want to be, where they can flourish, is crucial in helping build the Involvement dimension of Climate. Equally, there is also a responsibility to help steer an individual away from a decision that would prove to be little more than 'leaping from frying pan to fire' (which may, of course be caused by their being Predispositionally Impulsive). This necessitates application of a number of behaviours, e.g. Developing Others, Independence and Concern for Impact.

Esteem presents an interesting situation in that it may impel effort to be effective at delivering all the competency behaviours because individuals will not want to be considered weak in their thinking, ineffectual in their influencing, non-deliverers, or imbalanced in their Self-management. Quite where the 'hot-spot' causal linkages lie will only materialise through discussion, feedback and coaching which, in some ways, creates a fascinating dichotomy, i.e. wanting to hear positive feedback but not wanting to be regarded as a failure. This may appear unduly complex, but the nature and structure of well-formed feedback sessions provides the opportunity for the individual to set out his views first and, in such situations, most people are quite honest. Exceptions are seen principally with those who are highly Confident, i.e. tantamount to being arrogant, or highly Self-Conscious.

The link between Predispositions and Motivations

The link between the Predispositions considered within Feelings and Self-Control and certain aspects of Power, Achievement and Status presents a range of possible behavioural outcomes. An individual wanting control and authority (Power), being strongly ambitious (Achievement) and conscious of his status, coupled with being Discontented and Self-Conscious, could be impelled to deliver behaviour that demonstrates a high level of personalised power, e.g. a 'command and control' approach; perhaps, the 'boss from hell'.

This would be entirely different from an individual who is much more Self-contained, is less ambitious and wants to be more inclusive and collaborative as well as being less bothered about their status. Such individuals may exhibit greater humility* and [47] but be less inclined to 'trample down' others in their pursuit of promotion.

If we consider the association between Power and Extroversion and Introversion, we can deduce that someone who is more Accepting is likely to have less leadership success than if he was predispositionally more Assertive, simply because he builds less candour and credibility. While the individual may well be more orientated towards Socialised Power, his success may be relatively limited in forging relationships with and influencing those above and alongside him.

Taking this a stage further, a person high in Power but low in Assertiveness and generally expressive in terms of Self-consciousness and Pessimism may have considerable difficulty delivering the behaviour that one would normally associate with high power motivation. However, that said, I have worked with individuals who have attained very senior managerial positions possessing such characteristics but who have learned to deliver alternative behaviours effectively. It incurs a great deal of hard work and, sometimes, 'the lid comes off' and the Predispositions re-surface, which can cause not inconsiderable problems, not just for the individuals concerned but for the organisations that they lead.

At the risk of repeating myself, the fundamental issue in all of this analysis of Predispositions is to remember that Predisposition is **NOT** behaviour!

Predisposition represents a preferred mode of behaviour that provides comfort and satisfaction when the individual has the opportunity to deliver it.

---

* In Good to Great, Jim Collins talks about 'Level 5 Leadership' encompassing humility and fierce resolve. GPI™ and GMI offer a highly effective means of measuring Level 5 leadership.

Conclusions

It may well be that an individual who has certain Predispositions never delivers the expected behaviours because the organisation restricts the opportunity to do so. Remember also that while I cite behavioural competencies as the most important factor in the 'soup' of faculties an individual brings to a job, lacking the requisite skills and industry knowledge will affect the degree to which certain behaviours can be practised, at least initially.

The behaviours provide the means to transfer between sectors and get to grips with the technicalities of the new business activity, including making the move from private to public sector, or vice versa. Consider an individual with high power and high radical thinking who would be predicted to deliver strategic thinking and change but is unable to do so because he does not understand the business and, as a consequence, does not gain credibility among his colleagues. This underlies the need for a period of intense learning when transferring between organisations at senior levels. I would argue that in possessing the critical competencies, combined with good intelligence and sound business acumen, the much vaunted 100-day honeymoon can be significantly reduced and, as a result, the new executive can rapidly acquire knowledge, build credibility and start having a meaningful impact. Knowing the complexion of the team he is entering, i.e. their Predispositions and Motivations, also provides hugely important information that enables him to understand likely strengths and weaknesses.

It is also important to recognise that the same behavioural competency can be underpinned by quite different Predispositions, and that the same Predisposition can result in a wide range of different behavioural outcomes. This is down to the complex interplay that exists between an individual's Predispositions, his professional knowledge or skills and the organisational Climate in which he operates. Consequently, the linkages I have outlined represent only the 'tip of the iceberg'. This is not to say that this range of inter-dependencies cannot be fully understand and appreciated. Rather, it is a case of appreciating that human nature, if you will, is complex and cannot be 'boiled down' to overtly simplistic explanation akin to horoscopes, with their same lack of statistical reliability and validity.

Leadership and management is a complex subject and it is almost entirely dependent upon other people to achieve anything. There is an abundant need, therefore, for leaders and managers to appreciate their people as fully as possible, but without an unwarranted scale of (psycho-) analysis that causes paralysis of momentum in a competitive market.

Perhaps the easiest way to remember the key points of this chapter is to revert to Kurt Lewin's 'equation', which I portrayed in the preceding Chapter, i.e. *delivered behaviour is a function of person and situation*. A great deal of the time, we are able to deliver behaviour that emanates from our own natural style or Predisposition. The paramount point of importance is that, whatever the type of organisation, the behaviour that is required at any given time is that required by the circumstance of the moment.

Consider any of my consultant colleagues who can, at one point in the day, be engaged with the most senior individuals in an organisation and later that same day be fronting a Focus Group with shop-floor staff. It has not been unknown to be with a Chief Executive in the morning and with a Sister from a religious order in the afternoon. For either to deliver only their Predispositional make-up in either situation would result in a poor outcome. The have to 'act out' their learned behaviours.

Our approach to management development, therefore, can be seen as helping individuals to learn and subsequently deliver behaviours that are *out of character*, i.e. not their natural style.

An alternative way of describing the purpose of management development is that of it being the business of helping leaders and managers learn to do well what they are not good at.

CHAPTER 7:

Changing behaviour and making performance happen

My colleagues and I have helped leaders and managers in numerous organisations change and develop their behaviours in order to improve the performance of their organisation. As discussed in Chapter 1, this is typically measured by 'bottom line growth', either profit in the commercial sector or increased surplus in the public sector. Sometimes, our involvement has improved the bottom line, but in terms of reducing the deficit position.

The previous chapters outlined our methodologies and frameworks in quite some detail. However, our work is not just simply research but is far more about the practical application of our methodologies in modern organisations. We firmly believe in Lewin's assertion that "There is nothing as practical as a good theory"[48]. In our experience, participants in management development appreciate substance and validity and, therefore, care about the research underpinnings of the methodologies to which they are being exposed. Effective line-managers are not stupid; they recognise good development practices from the mediocre and will determinedly apply the former but reject the latter (when the 'training manual' sits on the shelf and gathers dust). They actually enjoy quality training interventions.

Our byword, therefore, is *"valid and practical".*

To amplify this fact, in this chapter I describe a number of actual case studies where our intervention has led to improved organisational performance. These add to the case study provided at the conclusion to Chapter 3.

Before I do this, it is useful to revisit the Integrated Framework, which was described earlier in this book (replicated in Figure 7.1).

The Integrated Framework lies at the heart of all we do. It indicates that changing leadership and team behaviour within the context of the organisation's structural design, and management of processes, results in enhanced Climate, which causes performance to improve.

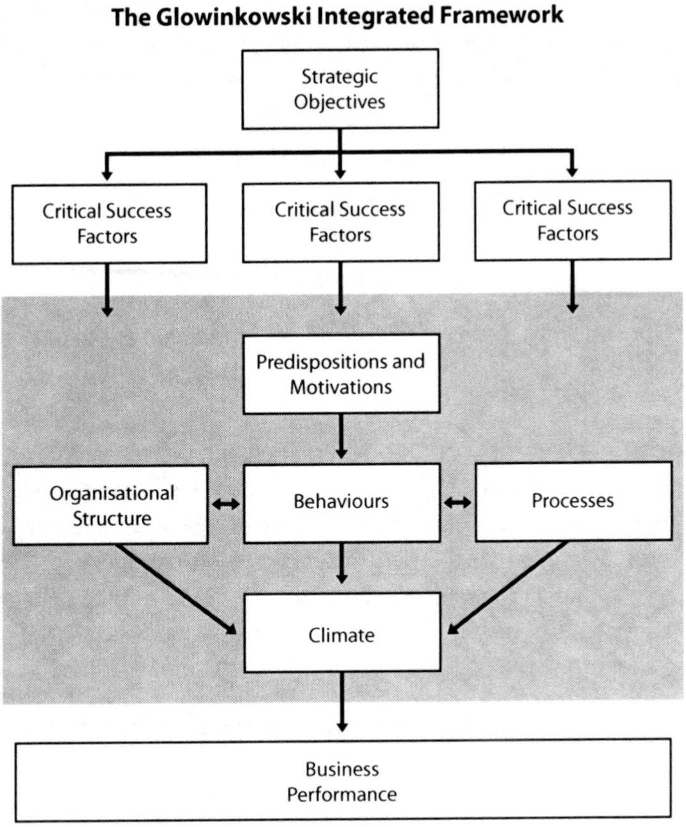

The Glowinkowski Integrated Framework

Figure 7.1

The model also shows that behaviour represents a bridge between intent, i.e. strategic objectives, and measured performance. Without that bridge in place there is no chance for an organisation to achieve its overarching goals and objectives.

A critical factor in each of the case studies that follows is the fact that measured improvements were achieved. The old adage that, "You can't change something if you are unable to measure it" is entirely apposite. All of the concepts described in this book thus far have been developed specifically with measurement very much in mind. Furthermore, that measurement is feasible creates the opportunity for individuals and teams to benchmark themselves against each of the components of the Integrated Framework. When working at one major UK bank, the salutary learning was not that the business unit was 'best of breed' internally, but that it was 'mid-table' against all the other organisations in our database at the time. (The best was a manufacturing business in Malaysia, by the way.) This galvanized the leadership team to incept a programme of change designed to drive up performance as measured across the full gamut of the business' balanced scorecard.

Progress depends on three things;

1. knowing where you are setting off from

2. knowing where you are trying to get to

3. possessing a means of sound and valid measurement to track progress

All too frequently, immense effort is spent on defining the second of these points, often described as the vision. However, there is little hope of arriving at the desired destination if the starting point is not known. The Chinese philosopher Confucius may have said, "A journey of a thousand miles begins with a single step." [49] However, if that step is in the wrong direction because of a failure to truly understand the starting point of the journey, it and all subsequent 999 steps will take the individual leader, their team and their organisation further away from their 'vision'.

What I describe in many of the following case studies is the means by which organisations and individuals have accurately defined from where they are starting their respective journeys. The result has been successful attainment of their defined goals.

Case Study 1

B-2-B and B-2-C decorative distribution business: 2001 to 2003

The business

The simple background to this situation was that one of the managers from a previous intervention was promoted to the position of General Manager (GM) of this business. Following his experience of the performance improvement opportunities achieved through a previous intervention, he was enthusiastic to repeat the process in his new enterprise.

The organisation comprised a distribution network of outlets across the UK serving professional tradesmen and the public. Although profitable, the business was facing considerable competitive pressure from the large DIY 'warehouse' businesses. There was also a sense that the organisation presented itself to the wider group as being 'sleepy' and that it was resting on its past laurels. In 2001, profit around £16 million.

Issues to be addressed

The new General Manager wanted to obtain the same level of detailed measurement as he had received before, which enabled action to be taken that drove change and business improvement. He wanted to waken the business. Also, the GM recognised that the participative nature of our approach brought about buy-in much more quickly than any other approach he had experienced, much enforced by the parent group.

The organisational structure included wide bands of control, e.g. managers' spans of control exceeded two dozen or more reports, which negated effective communication of the business' long-term direction[*] and imposed many logistical difficulties in exercising sound and effective managerial leadership in terms of performance and development review. External assessment showed that customers were becoming less aware of the business in its primary market segments.

---

[*] In another organisation, a manager we worked with talked about the need to "keep the red paint red" when communicating the long-term direction. Deviation and dilution of the message rendered the message ineffective and, as a result, the long-term direction was understood to relate to many points of the compass rather than a singular, unifying committed direction.

The intervention

In 2001, over a two-week period, using the Leadership for Organisational Improvement (LOI™) methodology, the business' senior leaders generated a change agenda to which they gave their highest level of commitment. The change agenda focused on enhancing their capability to manage the three change levers of structure, leadership behaviour and processes over the next couple of years.

Business outcomes

The consequential outcome from this intervention was simple.

- In 2003, the business' profit was £36 million, up from £16 million in 2001

The General Manager remarked, "I would never have believed that a *HR led intervention* could have had such a dramatically rich and positive business benefit. Without doubt, this program was the basis and catalyst for our exceptional increase in profitability."

From our perspective, we find in many organisations that HR is a 'whipping-post' function. Here is incontrovertible evidence of the impact that a HR function, which is business-focused and aware, can have upon its 'host' organisation.

If HR is not adding value in this manner to your organisation, it should be. If it isn't, it is nothing more than a cost burden managing 'pay and rations' and is ripe for outsourcing!

Case Study II

Financial Services organisation (Fund Management / Asset Management): late 1990s to 2004

The business

This financial services business was involved in asset management; it sold an extensive range of pension and investment products, which necessitated that a significant part of its activities was in fund management. When we worked with the business, it was part of a major UK bank.

The business had been a long standing player in its UK markets and its single, principal distribution channel was a Contact Centre.

Issues to be addressed

Business performance was poor.

- Staff turnover approached 40%, which, at the time, was high within the financial services contact centre sector; the average for the industry was just below 30%.

- It was difficult to recruit staff because of location, so the Contact Centre was often under resourced.

- Service levels and sales performance were both poor.

- The Contact Centre's management were considered to possess poor commercial acumen.

The paramount aim of our intervention was to try initially to resolve the turnover and recruitment problem.

The intervention

Leading up to the millennium, we delivered three principal interventions:

1. During 1998, we delivered our Development of Potential (DOP™)* process to the business' executive and senior management population. This was cascaded into the Contact Centre down to team leader level.

   DOP™ is a thorough assessment of an individual's behavioural competency profile, which provides comprehensive feedback to both the interviewee and their line manager.

   In this particular context, the core objective of DOP™ was to educate managers about behavioural competencies and enable each one to set out and agree with their manager a clear and concise programme of behavioural development that would result in delivery of improved performance, e.g. their teams would deliver better service and higher sales, as well as fulfilling their managerial obligations, e.g. compliance adherence, performance management and coaching, far more effectively.

2. An organisational specific Behavioural Competency Framework was developed, which defined and described the specific distinguishing behaviours that characterised outstanding performance in sales and service.

3. The Contact Centre leadership community underwent a programme to train them to performance manage using competencies, which was called 'Coaching for Competency'.

Business outcomes

By the end of 1999 the following, dramatically improved results were being delivered:

1. Through remote and direct call monitoring, a substantial improvement in the level of observed sales and service behaviour by Advisors was achieved.

---

* DOP™ is an individual assessment and feedback process that helps individuals establish a clear sense of where they sit against an international behavioural benchmarking framework based around our generic competency framework, which was described in Chapter 4. The process is explained more fully in Chapter 8.

2. Sales achieved to calls received ratios moved from 1:24 (pre-January 1999 figures) to 1:12, i.e. a 100% improvement.

3. Referral business increased by 150%.

4. Labour turnover reduced from its very high level to below 17% over the course of 12 months. Subsequent follow up work showed that over the following four years, turnover remained at about 16%.

5. Customer satisfaction ratings, as measured by MORI (now Ipsos MORI), showed that in January 1999 just 55% of customers were very satisfied. At the end of that year, the figures showed 89% to be very satisfied and, by mid-2000, the surveys showed 96% of customers to be very satisfied.

6. The businesses position in its market league table went from 12th (out of 14) to 2nd during 1999 and, by mid-2000, it had attained 1st position, displacing First Direct.

The most significant, substantial and immediate bottom-line performance increase emerges as a result of leadership behaviour change.

Case Study III

Retail distribution and service recovery: 1998 - 2005

The business

This was a large retail distribution business developing its capability to sell to and service its customers through contact centres. At the time, call centres were morphing into contact centres as telephony became integrated with other elements of nascent e-delivery. Initial work in a contact centre based in NW England resulted in our being asked to roll out our methodologies across three other centres with the intent to manage capacity within those centres and so avoid opening a fifth unit. Each centre was managed discretely.

Issues to be addressed

Forming a single, unified Direct Channels business from an array of previously discrete businesses, all operating their own HR practices, presented myriad challenges and difficulties.

The new Executive team responsible for managing this new channel wanted to achieve a consistent Climate across its different locations and a sense of real affinity to the business' brand first rather than local location. Furthermore, there were productivity and efficiency goals to achieve by centralising operations of the different centres into a single virtual entity.

In another arena, the group had decided to establish a new team at its Head Office to manage complaints addressed to its Chairman, CEO and Board Directors. It believed this new team would enable a far more consistent view of customer dissatisfaction to be obtained and that this feedback could help inform the organisation's change agenda.

The intervention

As a result of the successful implementation of our methodologies in the NW of England, we were invited to develop and implement a behavioural competency based performance management system. This entailed:

1. Developing a competency framework that could be used by all levels of management in recruitment, selection, performance management, development and succession planning.

2. Providing extensive 'Train the Trainer' skills transference to both line management and HR communities, so the processes listed in the preceding point could be managed jointly by both functions, in order to build collective responsibility.

3. Conducting DOP™ assessments with the upper two tiers of leadership and management for two purposes:

   a. To support appointments into a new organisational structure that we had designed.

   b. To support ongoing succession planning and talent development.

At group level, a team event examined collective team behaviours and individual Predispositions, and was coupled with an analysis of individual team members' competencies through conducting DOP™. The aim was to get a new team, operating in an entirely new context, to optimise its performance as quickly as feasible. Also, a second intent was to create a Climate that could support a team that was continually dealing with highly emotional and often aggressive customers.

Business outcomes

In the three other contact centres outside of NW England where we originally worked, the sales and service performance quickly improved to be on par with the first centre. Our surveys indicated much improved Climate, especially in terms of Clarity, Recognition and Involvement. Productivity, efficiency, effectiveness all improved to the extent that a fifth centre was not needed, which enabled earmarked investment to be re-directed to provide more extensive staff training and recognition.

At group level, feedback from customers who had complained indicated they were very pleased with how their complaints had been managed. Despite the mental rigour of the work, the Climate in the team was highly positive.

More critically, the growth in volume of complaints to the team was staunched because the feedback started to be used to invoke improvements to sales and service processes and practices. A real financial gain was calculated through measuring the reduction in the 'cost of re-work' that had to be undertaken in putting right mistakes. A comprehensive and consistent appreciation for the cost of re-work was acquired across the wider business.

Crucially, from a financial perspective, Direct Channels avoided having to open another contact centre.

At group level, enhancing cognizance of critical information overcame previous reluctance to invest in systems and staff education.

Case Study IV

Client services administration: 2002 to 2005

The business

This was a client services department of a London based investment management business dealing with personal, corporate and intermediary clients, i.e. brokers.

Issues to be addressed

The business was delivering poor performance, contributed to and compounded by high staff turnover, which was approaching 50%, which resulted in very low level morale as reported by the staff survey.

Staff recruitment was difficult because the high turnover set an adverse 'reputational tone' in the recruitment market; it was regarded as the last place to go and work.

There was a significant back-log of customer enquiries to be dealt with, which resulted in many complaints and considerable customer anger being vented at staff, which was the single-most explained reason why staff left. It was at risk of breaching compliance rules governing complaint handling.

It was a vicious circle.

The intervention

There were two principle elements:

1. A qualitative audit comprising a series of Focus Groups that sought to elicit staff's views of the business' capability within the main elements of the Integrated Framework. This provided clear and unambiguous information to the management population, which helped them understand their culpability in the business experiencing the issues it did and quickly won their hearts and minds to do something about it.

2. Development of an organisation specific Behavioural Competency

Framework and subsequent training of managers to use this in both selection and coaching contexts.

Business outcomes

Within nine months, the organisation had achieved year-on-year savings of £3 to £4 million pounds, which was accomplished through a relatively bloodless head count reduction. In this sort of context, we tend to find individuals either feel highly motivated to stay in the 'brave new world', i.e. a high performance culture, or to recognise that it is not for them and they de-select themselves by not applying for roles in the new organisational structure.

- The business moved from 14th out of 14 in a MORI customer satisfaction benchmarking survey to 5th position.

- The backlog of unaddressed queries was dramatically reduced.

Seeking early wins in terms of grabbing the 'low hanging fruit' is not to be under-estimated. These achievements enabled the business to move onto further and more dramatic performance improvement gains.

Case Study V

"Just a pair of hands": 2002

The situation

Georgina (not real name) had joined a project four months earlier before we started to work with her. Undoubtedly, it was an important project because:

- It was sponsored by the organisation's Chief Executive.

- It was managed overall by the Chief Operating Officer (COO).

- Nine months down the track, with another two years to run, the project comprised a team of 30 highly qualified practitioners in their field.

However, Georgina already had some concerns about success being less than guaranteed.

- There hadn't been a full project team meeting since she had joined, albeit the incidence of summer holidays had made that difficult.

- She had only really got to know the immediate few she worked with, and found it hard to find out what everyone else was doing and who to talk to about what.

In other words, there was low Clarity and poor Involvement.

The work Georgina was doing was interesting but she didn't feel that she had a specific area of responsibility she could call her own, where she could make decisions and have a bit of scope to influence things.

She sensed low Autonomy. Once or twice already, she had been asked to pass something she was working on to someone else; although they had said in each case it wasn't to do with the quality of her work. She didn't really know why the change had been made or what messages were being sent.

When she thought about it, she wasn't totally clear where her work fitted or what it was they were looking for from her. She was starting to feel that she was there primarily as 'just a pair of hands' and that it wasn't her ideas they were interested in.

She didn't feel fully involved or that she was part of the team yet.

She was scheduled to have a meeting with her manager to review progress but didn't want to 'rock the boat' but felt that she ought to say how she felt. She wanted to exercise Independence with appropriate Concern for Impact.

The intervention

We spent time coaching Georgina and helping her to think through the situation and to prepare how to present her thoughts to her boss, the COO. The following suggestions were made and accepted by Georgina:

- To discuss with the COO her role in detail, clarifying expectations and agreeing clear areas of responsibility; this helped Georgina to understand her particular role in the change programme.

- To deliver a weekly, verbal report to the COO, which would replace the daily written report previously sought. The weekly report would look at progress made and any key issues arising and provide more time for Georgina's ideas to be discussed. If anything critical arose during the week, Georgina could 'pop her head round the door' and discuss them straight away. The intent was to move to interactive discussion rather than bland, repetitive reporting.

- The project plan would be displayed in full on the COO's wall; each work group would be responsible for making sure its entry was up-to-date and show clearly who was currently working on what.

- Georgina was to influence and win commitment from the rest of the team to regular full team meetings at which each work group would have time to present their work and have it reviewed by everyone else. The intent was to ensure clear line of sight through all activities towards the end goal.

Outcomes

As a result of these actions, Georgina and her colleagues felt much clearer about the overall aims of their project, particularly where their work fitted into the overall organisation's much wider strategic intentions.

Everyone felt clearer about their respective responsibilities and how performance would be tracked and reviewed.

Georgina and her peers felt collectively that they could each influence the end-goal more effectively, particularly in terms of taking a far more collaborative approach.

In Climate terms, Clarity improved, as well as Autonomy, Recognition and Involvement. The project delivered ahead of schedule, to budget and pay-back was achieved three months ahead of the projected time-line.

Identifying the right behavioural approach to broach a difficult situation resulted in improvements to the team's collective behaviours, enhanced Climate, and, thereby, better performance.

Case Study VI

A Downward Spiral: 2006

The situation

When Linda (name changed) was appointed as head of function, the team had been together for several years. As with most teams there had been many changes over the years, many of which had been driven by the need to cut cost by changing organisational structures, e.g. de-layering, rationalisation.

There were no real problems in the team as such, though there was a general sense of people protecting their own niches, being reluctant to propose changes and exercise little effort supporting other members of the team. There also tended to be very little sharing of expertise between team members.

- In Climate terms, there was low Change Orientation and Involvement.

Although there were few complaints from the customers, there were not many positive comments either. The work load on the team was increasing and this tended to push anything that was not day-to-day into the background. Whenever the group sat down for a meeting, most of the time was spent discussing day-to-day problems rather than getting down to identifying and planning improvements to customer service.

- There was low Directional behaviour.

Linda was aware that a lot of fairly routine problems were being referred to her whenever people ran into difficulty.

- There was low Positional behaviour.

Linda came to the conclusion that steps would have to be taken to reverse a prospectively more damaging downward spiral.

The intervention

We coached Linda to initiate the following prioritised actions:

- To talk to a number of her key customers to find out what kind of service they were looking for from the team and how they expected it to change in the future.

- To talk to each of the team members in turn to find out how they spent their time currently, what parts of the team's work they had experience of, and how they would like to see their roles develop.

- To arrange a day away from the office for the whole team where we facilitated a structured discussion around what the team needed to do to satisfy the changing needs of the customers.

- To encourage the team to identify a list of improvements that could be made in the way they worked. Many frustrations came to the surface. Linda encouraged people to openly discuss their concerns.

Business outcomes

As a consequence, Linda established a number of small groups to plan how to make progress on the key areas identified by the team.

- The work areas were re-organised so that people were clearly responsible for all aspects of service for a specific customer group. This meant that people needed to share their expertise with each other.

- Systems and processes were set up to ensure people had access to the know-how they required, both via IT, i.e. a knowledge management system, and sharing of personal expertise.

- Team members set themselves specific performance management goals to spend time training each other and to ensure such skills transfer was effective, i.e. the learner could exercise the learnt skills.

This allowed the team to be more flexible and prompt in their response to customer needs; their productivity and efficiency as well as their effectiveness all increased, i.e. more was done with the same resource and it was done correctly first time.

- Ways were found to increase the level of responsibility for each team member, i.e. jobs were enlarged and enriched. In some cases, work was eliminated by finding simpler ways to do things, fewer mistakes were being made so errors were not having to be put right, and in other situations, part-time staff were allocated the routine work that could be completed within their shifts, eliminating the need for handovers, which were found to be a key source of mistakes.

- The managers in the team were able to spend more of their time working on improvement activities to provide a better service to the customers. As a result, everyone, including the customers, agreed that the standard of service had improved.

- The release of time back to the managers from not getting sucked into the 'nitty-gritty' allowed them to work more closely with their team members on performance management and coaching. The 'performance bar' was continually being lifted.

- Team meetings were subsequently able to concentrate on monitoring progress in numerous change initiatives that were under way.

In looking back after six months, the team agreed that it was now providing a much better standard of service, and it also had the external research measurement to corroborate this. The group considered they were much more flexible and responsive in the way it handled customers' requests and dealt with change, which they themselves incepted. People both acknowledged and liked the fact that their responsibilities had grown and the jobs were more interesting. Inter-team co-operation within the overall group was far better; the old silos had been demolished.

Influencing is an all too easily forgotten performance criterion of leadership. We consider it to be the most important area because most things necessitate the involvement of others and winning hearts and minds is vital to achieving success.

Case Study VII

A chemical business; two teams, two different cultures: 1997 - 1999

The business

This case study involved two different businesses working in a quasi-joint venture scenario, which involved a major UK based chemical company selling part of its chemical manufacturing process to a US based company.

The deal was not without its complexities because the US company had become both supplier to and customer of the UK company. Additionally, there were performance targets relating to the volume and the quality of chemicals being sold between the two businesses. Quite quickly, dissatisfaction and litigious disagreement arose between both companies.

We became involved in the context of 'corporate marriage guidance counsellors' where relationships between the two senior management teams of the respective companies had entirely broken down. For instance, in early telephone conversations with one of the American executives, he expressed profane enmity about the lack honesty and a sense of duplicity when dealing with his UK counterpart. Equally, it is recalled a UK participant in the venture feeling continuously brow beaten and dispirited following many difficult meetings.

The challenge was to overcome these feelings of ill-will and develop a more effective set of collaborative and collegiate relationships between the managers in order to build trust, openness and engagement. If this were achieved, the joint venture could operate on a level above basic adherence to an extremely complex and rigid legal contract. The UK business' survival depended upon this being achieved.

The intervention

The intervention focused on helping the individuals think about their own respective styles and how these would help build co-operation or generate conflict. The GPI™ questionnaire was completed by all the managers and the resultant data was fed back to them in a workshop process.

The GPI™ profiles for the two Chief Executives and their respective teams were enormously revealing. Using the Communication and Inter-personal Style feedback model, it was clear that the US team were essentially Challenger in nature, while the UK team sat across the Supporter and Encourager styles. That these Predispositions were being delivered as actual behaviours totally accounted for the different views we had heard expressed, including those incidents mentioned just before:

- The UK management team described their US colleagues as aggressive, abrasive and coercive in their style.

- In contrast, the US colleagues described their UK counterparts as entirely unprepared to face up to difficult issues and would tend to agree at meetings but then go off and "do their own thing".

One comment made by the UK Chief Executive paints a vivid picture, "Sometimes, I just feel a complete lack of energy in reacting to Nick's (name changed) abrasive style. I guess I just engage in the meeting and then, when it's over, we can go on and get on with our real job."

It is easy to see from this combination of styles why the US individuals would essentially perceive their UK colleagues to be somewhat deceptive in their approach; yet, really this was not the point. We had unearthed the classic example of two different *cultures* that recruited people using a variety of weak recruitment practices that essentially did no more than recruit in the corporate likeness; behaviours and impact on Climate were not considered.

In sharing the GPI™ data at the workshop and facilitating discussion about what it was inferring enabled the surfacing of differences within the relationships between the two groups of managers. There is no doubt that when people began to see the significance of these different styles and how they could impact actual behaviours their perceptions towards each other began to change. People felt more comfortable and easy with each other because they appreciated why they were behaving as they did.

There was a similar dichotomy when the Problem Solving and Implementation was scrutinised.

- The US individuals' data was skewed towards the Visionary style.

- Their UK counterparts were mainly in the Planner or Practitioner quadrants.

The split between the teams was re-emphasised even more when the managers were asked to overlay the two sets of data and start to consider how "Visionary / Challengers" could get along with "Planner / Encouragers".

The challenge was considerable but not insurmountable.

Business outcomes

As a result of the intervention, the teams' awareness of their respective styles was made conscious and, therefore, they had a base on which they could consider how to operate differently, i.e. they knew why people did what they did and why they reacted in the way that they did.

By itself, we wouldn't go as far as to claim that using the GPI™ in this way fixed the problem; it isn't the proverbial magic, pixie dust. Any consultancy intervention is like 'taking a horse to water'. You can get it there, but you can't force it to drink!

What is clear is that on subsequent visits to the organisation, the mood was more relaxed and there was far more willing and warmer dialogue occurring between the previously disparate factions.

Over time, the joint venture got itself back on track due mainly to the managerial population recognising they needed to act and behave differently to create a true, high-performance Climate.

Case Study VIII

The immovable object and the irresistible force: 2003 - 2004

The business

After the turn of the millennium, a financial services organisation decided to merge two of its businesses. The rationale for this exercise was the promise of significant cost savings and the opportunity of presenting itself to the market as a single, unified entity, which offered the prospect of considerable cross-selling between the respective business' customer groups. The strategy appeared sound, yet two-and-a-half years after the merger, no real cost savings had been made and cross-sales were not occurring either.

The intervention

As a result of other work we had conducted earlier within the parent group, we possessed the GPI™ profiles for over 50 senior managers from each of the respective organisations.

Figures 7.2 and 7.3 below illustrate the patterns of shapes within both the Problem Solving and Implementation, and Communication and Inter-personal style models. Over the two frameworks we saw:

- Business A was dominated by a combination of Planners and Independent/Supporter groups; by profession many were accountants and/or from an insurance background.

- By comparison, Business B was dominated by Visionary and Encourager types; they tended to be involved in service and sales delivery in retail banking.

Problem Solving and Implementation Style

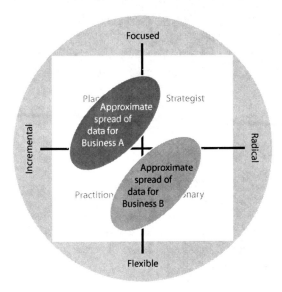

Figure 7.2

Communication and Inter personal Style

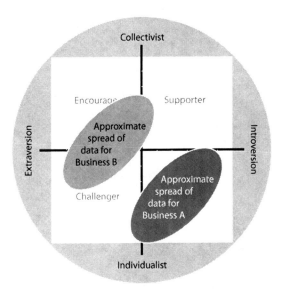

Figure 7.3

Upon reflection, we viewed this as unsurprising because these Predispositions are to be expected in these respective contexts. We find many people who go into retail banking have chosen not to go to university and often express their rationale for their career decision as an opportunity to work with customers and to join a team that they feel good about being in. In contrast, our experience in organisations such as Business A evidences a strong proportion of people who are good at maths, go through university taking maths or accountancy degrees and then seek a career as actuaries or in insurance underwriting; they want to continue to be able to analyse and work independently.

Behavioural and business outcomes

The key point, of course, is the fact that the combination of styles arising from the different cultural backgrounds that we describe causes considerable difficulties in working out how to retain the best qualities of both organisations and overcome those more discordant issues.

While the merged organisation began to achieve its goals, this case study is cited to make another critical point. Once an Executive team has decided to buy, acquire or merge another organisation, it is essential that in parallel with the financial due diligence, a comprehensive managerial due diligence exercise is conducted. The knowledge so acquired, be it at the level of Predispositions or Competencies, will help the new management team come together and start to work effectively more quickly than if they started out not knowing each others' styles and methods of working.

Case Study IX

Application of GPI™ in building a high-performance team: 2006 - 2008

The business

The organisation was a specialist division of a global manufacturing organisation that provided products and services to people from the country where it was based who were living and working within Europe and UK.

Issues to be addressed

The client had previously used GPI™ as part of a team building process to ensure that a rapidly formed team came together and operated well. Over time, as it was necessary to recruit new team members, the client wanted to ensure that:

- The 'shape' of the team continued to be balanced in terms of types of people

- Each individual displayed both the right behaviours , technical competence but also 'profile' necessary to most successful in their role

This was partially as a result of a previous experience where an individual had joined the team before the above approach was put into place. That individual is struggling with the role, and there are clear signs that the degree of outcome focus and relationship building aspects of the role are not being achieved. The GPI™, had it been examined, makes that quite clear as to a possible danger.

For that reason, the client wanted to use GPI™ as supportive data for new hires.

The intervention

We supported the client by ensuring new candidates completed the GPI™. Those clients went through an interview process initially (both with the business head and HR business partner). From that data, a short list was developed, and then we held discussions with the client regarding the profile we saw.

Typically, we used the GPI™ profile to match against the job role requirements, and highlight those areas where there could be some pressures for the individual to perform the role well.

In one particular case there were two candidates for a Relationship Management role, where there were, inter alia, two key requirements:

- The need to manage relationships well at all levels, internally and externally, and with a degree of humility and caution

- The need to be in-role for around two years in order to foster and nurture those relationships

In this particular case, candidate A was the client's initial preferred choice. The reason was they performed well in the interview, with confidence, and portrayed a command of what they could bring to the role.

Candidate B, whilst strong was, in the client's view, just pipped to the post as they were not coming across as keen and as strong in the interview.

Candidate A was interviewed in person by the business head, and Candidate B was interviewed over the telephone.

The data was fascinating.

They both shared a similar profile as regards their desire for results and good outcomes, and a level of conceptualisation needed in the role.

However when it came to the Communications and interpersonal style, there were significant differences. In the main, this related to the degree of extraversion, assertiveness and the dissenting nature of Candidate A over Candidate B. It was clear that at times Candidate A could be 'in your face', and whilst this bubbly nature was good in some roles, this particular role required greater control, care and humility as was presented in Candidate B.

The other significant factor was around Impulsiveness. Candidate A was highly impulsive, and as a result had a low boredom threshold. Candidate B was the opposite. As a result, there would have to be doubts as to whether or not candidate A would last the two years required in the role. Indeed the evidence of the CV affirmed this fact with seven roles in six years!

On the basis of those discussions, the client changed their mind and opted for

Candidate B. They are now in the team and performing well.

Indeed, when we provided feedback to candidate A on why they did not get the role, and we pointed out these factors, they absolutely agreed, and indeed confirmed that it would have been unlikely they would have stayed a year, and was thinking that a marketing role was more suited to them!

Conclusion

The result has been a well sorted team, in so far that each person has been brought in with a best match as possible to the nature of their role, so they can play significantly to their strengths, yet still have opportunity to develop and stretch themselves in some areas.

It has also meant that the overall team shape has been blended to get a good balance of type, so whenever there is a particular issue at stake, they can draw upon the people who have a natural aptitude to operate in that area.

Without this approach, the client believes that they would have struggled with recruitment and creating a high performing team.

Case Study X

Developing a competency framework for high performance for front line agents in global, complex call centres: 2005 to 2008

The business

This was the principal service delivery function of an organisation delivering specialised services to an eclectic mix of corporate clients in a multi-lingual environment.

Issues to be addressed

The client was suffering with a relatively high level of turnover of front line agents, exacerbated by the location of other competitors nearby and so a migrant, fickle workforce. In addition, there was a drive to try and improve performance in an area where the word 'service' and 'customer' had only really been recently accepted, and clearly in the eyes of some, not enforced!

We had already undertaken some work with the client and they asked if we could look at this area with an objective to help identify what it was about the higher performers that made the difference, which all others could then aspire to. Additionally, they wanted to help Team Leaders know who were high performers and, critically, why. This would help them in their provision of feedback and coaching to help others improve their performance.

The intervention

We undertook a piece of significant research that:

- Examined groups of high performers, and what it was about those individuals that made a difference, behaviourally

- Examined those individuals' motivational drivers and also their predispositions to identify common themes

- Compared this to a 'control group that were low/medium performers

The research was undertaken using questionnaires, focus groups and 1-2-1 interviews.

One of the interesting findings was the degree to which high performers were disgruntled with leaders who tolerated poor performance within the team, as inevitably it fell to the high performers to back-fill!

There were two key outcomes that arose from this research.

One was the way in which the GPI™ and could be used for 'profiling' the type of individuals that is best attracted in the role for that kind of environment (for example it is an environment where there is a need for higher levels of personal robustness, and a real drive for results delivery). This profiling was then developed into an approach for recruitment.

The second was the creation of a competency framework for the agents, which showed there were eight key behavioural competencies necessary to perform well in the role, and which the high performers all displayed. For example, the critical, anchor competency was that of 'Client Thinking', i.e. getting into the head of the client. While this sounds obvious, it transpired that there were a number of individuals who were simply not comprehending what the client was seeking, let alone empathising with them. This was a key differentiator between higher and mediocre performance.

However, having a framework alone was not sufficient. What was critical was the need for every team leader to understand it, and use it effectively as part of their performance management discussions with their team members.

We implemented an approach that took groups of team leaders through a very practical process to understand the links of behaviours to performance and importantly to practice how to have the conversation with a member of their team.

At the end of the implementation, every leader had a process to follow and greater confidence in how to handle those discussions, in particular some of the difficult discussions that can occur.

There was also a very useful by-product from this process, and that was an assessment of the capability across the management population as regards:

- Talent and potential

- Poorer performers who were clearly 'at risk' within the role and indeed damaging to their team

Conclusion

There were three broad conclusions from this work.

1. The first was the creation of a common language within a robust framework that could drive performance which managers and staff alike could relate to as being real, pertinent and applicable to their role. Its 'ease' and the fact there were only eight core competencies for the majority of staff was well received and made life simple.

2. The second was that the client had to think carefully about investing real time to make this stick, as it is not a one-off approach. As a consequence we trainer trained individuals within the organisation to ensure they had self sufficiency and sustainability to continue the work of embedding the approach across the business.

3. The final area was around the capability of the management that became evident from this exercise – and we helped the client understand the 'bell' curve of performance across those managers. From that there were some real success stories including the very quick promotion of one their top performers who we rated highly. In addition, there were some individuals who, realising this was not the job for them, then de-selected themselves and asked to be moved. In a couple of other cases managers were performance managed out, as they simply could not rise to the demands of the leadership role.

Overall therefore, the client ended up with a clear framework for managing and sustaining performance, and that is still evident today.

Case Study XI

Providing direction for a new Academy: 2007 to 2008

The business

On this occasion, 'the business' was a secondary school in S.E. England, which opened as a flagship Academy in September 2007. As is the case with Academies, the school was "sponsored" by an external body, in this case, a local Further Education College (FE).

In its previous incarnation, the school was one of the worst performing in the country. In the academic year immediately prior to the school becoming an Academy, fewer than one in five of its pupils (18%) had attained 5 GCSE grades of A*- C, the critical indicator for school performance at 15-16 years. This placed it in the bottom 1% of schools.

The school's catchment area is one of high economic and social deprivation. Parental support is not especially strong. It is under the flight path to an airport, so pupils have to contend with noise and pollution.

Issues to be addressed

The school's Principal was appointed during summer 2007. He was the sixth person to occupy the role in the past four years. Expectations of pupils and parents were not great. A critical task centred on winning these stakeholders round to the vision which he and the Academy's sponsor had developed in their short time working together.

The FE's Chief Executive had a very clear vision. He believed that by sponsoring two Academies and building a strong, explicit link with his institution, greater educational opportunities and through these, life opportunities, could be provided to the young people of the town, which the schools and the FE served.

The Academy's leadership team inherited by the new Principal comprised managers from the old, failing school, plus an Associate Principal who had been recruited from another Academy and was highly regarded. The Principal and Assistant were determined to rejuvenate this team and enable them and their respective teams to achieve the demanding targets that had been set for them by the sponsor.

The intervention

Prior to the first workshop, the client spelt out his priority for the leadership team, namely that they needed to come away from the session with a stronger sense of self-belief and drive than he had experienced hitherto. He was adamant that there was considerable potential in the group. If they could dissociate themselves from the 'failing school' label that continued to haunt them, they could meet, if not exceed, their targets.

In its first year, the Academy's focus was predominantly tactical: results at GCSE had to improve, otherwise the sponsor's vision and, thereby, the credibility of the team, would suffer. Strategic considerations had taken second place thus far although the team recognised these could not be deferred indefinitely; they had to start thinking of year 2 and beyond.

Following a series of one-to-one feedback sessions debriefing the team members on their GPI™, we were asked us to conduct a 'Direction Setting Workshop'. On arrival, the team were apprehensive, unsure of precisely what lay in store for them. What became clear was that given a chance to express their ambition for the new Academy, and to dispel their frustrations with previous leaders, a positive energy could be generated. Understanding their differing predispositions and motivations provided a basis for some rich dialogue from which everyone acquired a new found appreciation of the differing perspectives and strengths around the table.

For the team to understand each others' GPI™ and GMI profiles enabled the team to exercise strong problem-solving focus, considering issues from a variety of angles. The more exuberant gave 'air-time' to the quieter members and everyone made an explicit contribution.

Business outcomes

In less than twelve hours of working time, a purpose statement and eight critical success factors were generated coupled with supporting action programmes for each of these eight areas of intended endeavour.

One of the Assistant Heads remarked at the end of the day that he felt he had been listened to and understood by the team for the first time in many years. Another team member remarked that she finally understood why she thinks like she does.

The Principal considered that the main impact of the intervention was to 'gel the team' in minimal time. (Indeed, we were well reminded of a previous intervention several years with another management team when the boss remarked how they had managed to do three years relationship building in three days.)

From qualitative discussions with staff, students and parents, the Principal is confident that there is far greater confidence in the Academy's leadership and management team. In parallel, systems and procedures are much more robust.

Finally, when the results were announced in the summer, they were spectacular. More than one in three (35%) achieved 5 or more A*-C (including English and Maths). On the broader definition, 41% achieved 5 or more, up from 19% the previous year.

Case study XII

A "gift" for the Sisters of a religious order: 2006 to 2008

It is appropriate to give brief mention to this intervention in light of the preceding one.

The business / Issues to be addressed

Our involvement in this 'business', this time a religious order of nuns, who are leaders of schools and charities supporting deprived teenagers, both of which are recognised as exceptionally difficult leadership situations. In one particular situation, two Sisters shared role reversal in their educational responsibilities to that which prevailed in their religious order, i.e. in a school, one was the boss, while in the order, the other was the boss.

The nuns had become aware of our business by virtue of our working with one of the schools in which they were involved through helping it to recruit a new head teacher. This opportunity had arisen through a manager in a corporate client being a School Governor and asking if the GPI™ could be used in the selection process. Like the school in the previous example, this school operated in very difficult circumstances and its exam performance was not especially strong. Demand for entry into its sixth form was falling away raising the spectre that this could be closed.

The nuns were interested in becoming trained to use GPI™ in their various 'managerial' activities as they believed it would help them appreciate colleagues better and to provide better coaching and developmental input to the people with which they worked.

The intervention

Over the course of a weekend, we trained a dozen members of the order to review, assess, assimilate GPI™ and conduct feedback sessions, both individual and team based.

Business outcomes

For the school recruiting a new Head using GPI™ helped them identify a more forward-thinking Head who was genuinely ambitious for the school's pupils and confident in her abilities to lead her team to deliver enhanced academic performance and improved pastoral support and encouragement. In her first year following appointment exam performance improved and demand for sixth form places grew. The school was successful in applying for Specialist Status in Arts and Drama, having previously unsuccessfully applied for other specialisms. The Head recognised that the pupils were keen on Arts and Drama (they wanted to become celebrities!). However, unimagined spin-off benefits were seen. Interest in and academic performance achieved in Science improved because the pupils wanted to know how their bodies functioned and in Geography, too, because they wanted to know more about the African sources of much of the music they listened to.

For the two nuns who were manager to each other in their different environments, GPI™ enabled them to appreciate their respective natural strengths and development needs and why their 'hierarchy' made sense in the different situations. Each has sparked off against the other more readily, reduced some sense of friction and intrusion. Each truly values what the other 'brings to the party' in terms of bolstering their collective capability in each situation.

All the nuns quickly mastered GPI™ and have employed it judiciously in their respective areas of leadership activity. They have particularly enjoyed helping young adults in their charge complete the questionnaire and provide them with feedback and build the sense of esteem and self-worth. They are seeing some really positive progression by these individuals where previously they had been 'written off' as having little or no potential.

We are especially proud of this work.

Case Study XIII

Enhancing relationships between members of an Executive team: 2004 to 2006

The business

This case study involves a major, global, industrial conglomerate with turnover exceeding US$30bn and employing around 450,000 employees.

Issues to be addressed

This piece of work focussed entirely on the issue of relationships among the executive team. In particular, there was concern that whilst the CEO was highly respected and regarded, his impact with senior colleagues was heavily reliant upon separate one-to-one discussions with the different directors. There was a general sense of belief that the organisation needed to change dramatically its culture from one of 'command and control' into one that provided opportunity for greater innovation, creativity and inclusiveness.

The critical objective was to improve and enhance the quality and effectiveness of the executive team meetings which took place.

The intervention

The executive team included the CEO and over 12 other directors. The work started with a series of one-to-one feedback and coaching sessions with each member of this team. It culminated in facilitating a variant of the Direction Setting Workshop.

Business outcomes

At a qualitative level there was clear evidence that improvements emerged as a result of the process. For instance, the CEO learnt that it was better for him not to give his opinion before asking a question; he needed to garner view and opinion from the team before making any remarks himself.

At a more quantitative level, it was clear that this workshop process was part of a broader catalyst, which helped established a powerful corporate-wide change agenda through the Directors collectively delivering enhanced Strategic Influencing behaviour. Their discussions distilled a cohesive and well co-ordinated programme of activities, which included major restructuring, the development of a competency framework and using this within the performance management processes to enhance the quality of behavioural delivery across the entire organisation.

With its activities crossing many sectors, the organisation enjoys a high level of respect for its financial performance and its ground-breaking corporate social responsibility activities.

Case Study XIV

Helping establish a new culture and enhanced climate: 2006 to 2007

The business

This business is a global manufacturer with annual turnover exceeding €6 billions and employing almost 40,000 people.

Issues to be addressed

The focus for this organisation was achieving an effective cultural change having moved to being organised by business activity from being structured around country activities. (As cited earlier in the book, for this culture change programme to be fully effective, it was critical that the 'people dimension' was not overlooked as, in our experience, is so often the case.) While the organisation demonstrated some the very positive, entrepreneurial characteristics, i.e. dynamism, market focus, etc., it also demonstrated a number of negative features such as poor understanding of the importance of having effective corporate structures and efficient managerial processes. Too much was regarded as being done on 'the back of a cigarette packet'.

The intervention

This intervention initially involved the business' executive team, but with a clear intent that this would be followed by a cascade into the wider leadership population.

Leadership behaviour was measured quantitatively and qualitatively. The measurement data was fed back in both workshop and one-to-one sessions with the seven members of the Executive. Although not explicitly measured, this enabled highly effective dialogue to be facilitated over a six-month period about the impact their individual and collective data had on the organisation's Climate.

As intended, this then provided the springboard to take the measurement, discussion and action planning deeper into the management population.

Business outcomes

Over the course of our involvement, we observed measurable shifts in the quality of leadership behaviour delivery. At a more qualitative level, the intervention enabled the executive team to shift its collective thinking and help build stronger risk mitigation and governance to underpin its entrepreneurial dynamism. The team recognised that as the business grew and manufactured a greater range of products distributed to a wider geographic reach that both structures and processes needed to be managed with greater focus in order to strengthen Climate and continue to its track record of profit growth.

Some re-structuring occurred, in which we were involved in the recruitment and selection process for some key new roles that were created. The organisation put in place a more inclusive planning process and actively encouraged two-way communication through using technology and more face-to-face engagement between the executives and their business functions, e.g. through 'Town Hall' sessions.

Case Study XV

Consolidating an organisation's position within the FTSE 500 and providing the platform for future growth: 2007 to 2008

The business

This is a business with an entrepreneurial background linked to the construction and property sectors. It employs over 500 people.

Issues to be addressed

The key issue here was to develop the executive team to be more open among themselves and so provide more effective operations leadership capability. Like the preceding case, albeit operating on a smaller 'canvas', the underlying business need was to help a highly entrepreneurial team become more professional in terms of its leadership capability through identifying and rectifying dysfunctional behaviours, of which a lack of openness was most prominent.

The intervention

This intervention started by examining the behaviours deployed by the Directors when engaging with the CEO and Deputy Chief Executive. It quickly became clear that the Directors exuded a lack of confidence in these interactions due to feeling somewhat inexperienced and, as a result, reporting relatively low esteem within the Feelings and Self-control framework of GPI™.

This behavioural review also highlighted that two senior executives needed to modify their approach in order to provide clearer, more succinct direction and, thereby, empowerment for their direct reports. They needed to tackle issues rather than avoid them.

A team workshop involving eight junior executives was facilitated in which they reviewed their GPI™ data and considered how their traits (and, as indicated above, their current self-rating) affected how they behaved towards each other and as a collective group. The resultant rich dialogue caused a level of candour to be created between the team, which was neither threatening nor intimidating for even the most self-critical and reserved participant.

Individual feedback discussions were held with each participant, followed by 'three-way' conversations including either the CEO or Deputy Chief Executive. Finally, the full team, including the CEO and his deputy, was convened in a Direction Setting Workshop event. This enabled the more unified group to establish a clear sense of purpose and to set out eight critical success factors and a range of personally allocated actions, which promoted a very clear sense of accountability and collaborative and mutually supportive commitment.

Business outcomes

Measurement of the team's behaviours was completed at the start and conclusion of the section of our intervention with this business. The degree of openness reported quantitatively and witnessed qualitatively was marked, even within a relatively short timeframe of six months. The quality of discussion at executive meetings became far more focused and oriented towards bringing the newly stated sense of purpose into reality. Of most note, was a marked increase in the sense of Clarity that pervaded the team and down into their respective functions of the business. Their management of critical processes sharpened through incepting a range of projects to review and refine communication and limits of authority within decision making. The team feel they are now far more prepared to contend with the economic upheavals affecting their primary business sectors.

The executive team have now approved a broad leadership development programme to involve the next levels of senior and middle managerial tiers, which will include a talent assessment audit and a training programme to enhance engagement skills.

Case Study XVI

Succession planning in a family owned organisation: 2007 to 2008

The business

This study involves a family owned business with a multi-million pound turnover and several thousand employees.

Issues to be addressed

Critically, the organisation wants to become far more 'commercially savvy' but not to lose the many positive attributes of being family owned, of which, perhaps, the most impressive characteristic is its focus on staff development. For the top 50 managers, the organisation wanted to develop a sharper leadership edge, which emphasises a performance culture.

The intervention

Our work commenced with the executive team, which comprised the CEO and seven Executive Directors. Each member of the team went through the DOP™ process, which provides a very significant coaching intervention for each individual and sets in place a clear development plan.

Following completion of these individual reviews, the full team were brought together for a three-day Direction Setting Workshop.

Business outcomes

All the qualitative assessment and quantitative measurement conducted prior to the workshop pointed towards a need to galvanize a greater sense of single purpose for the overall organisation and to dismantle fiefdoms that were more oriented towards local goals.

Observation showed that executive meetings became more objective and more purposefully managed with the resultant communication out to the wider business helping build greater transparency and an enhanced sense of Clarity about the organisation's longer-term aims and aspirations. The previously quite strong 'walls' that existed between functional silos began to be dismantled particularly in terms of recognising that enhanced Customer Understanding would enable the organisation to present a unique proposition to its widening reach into its market-place. Furthermore, a greater sense of innovation was instilled particularly in respect of defining plausible commercial opportunities within a burgeoning awareness of 'green' issues that was becoming much more starkly apparent across its immediate customer base and, more particularly, the shape of demand that was being fashioned within the ultimate end-user communities.

Summary and conclusions

Each of the case studies described in this chapter exemplify the critical composition and *theory* of the Integrated Framework. They clearly indicate the significance of behaviour and, in some cases, draw attention to the importance of how Predispositions underpin these behaviours in a very specific way.

Behaviours can be measured and, when reported through an intervention such as LOI™, demonstrate a clear and undeniable link with Climate. Such data gives an organisation a strong platform on which change can be orchestrated at the level of the individual, the team, function or business unit, and the whole organisation.

> **Once attention is paid by leaders to how they behave, how they assemble their businesses structurally and manage key organisational processes, Climate improves and, with it, performance.**

48 See Kurt Lewin's "Field theory in social science; selected theoretical papers", edited by D. Cartwright published in 1951

49 www.quotedb.com/quotes/1483

50 In another organisation, a manager we worked with talked about the need to "keep the red paint red" when communicating the long-term direction. Deviation and dilution of the message rendered the message ineffective and, as a result, the long-term direction was understood to relate to many points of the compass rather than a singular, unifying committed direction.

CHAPTER 8:

Weaving behaviour and Climate into the fabric of organisational life

The previous chapter provided a series of case studies where we were involved in helping individual managers and management teams to 'raise their game' and improve their performance. Perhaps the more important issue, however, concerns how organisational leaders can begin to adopt the thinking relating to Predispositions, behavioural competencies and Climate.

Learning and understanding the Integrated Framework and its constituent elements will result in these principles becoming the very fabric of organisational life. As a result, there will be a clear and distinctive appreciation that Climate, more than anything else, drives performance over a prolonged period. Other initiatives may give an organisation a 'sharp kick in the pants' (SKIP), but their impact peters away after a relatively short time. Concerted concentration of effort by leaders to improve their behaviours, to construct a robust yet flexible structure, and to manage efficient and effective processes will build a high-performance Climate that is sustainable.

This chapter explores the four key areas of application that constitute the critical domains of the HR management cycle, namely:

1. The selection and recruitment processes that the organisation adopts.

2. Using behaviour and competency as part of the performance management process.

3. Making behaviour, Climate and Predisposition a critical focus of learning and development.

4. Using competencies as part of the talent management and succession planning processes.

Configuring our methodologies to this cycle recognises the critical importance that people play in enabling organisations to achieve their aims. It brings HR to the 'wing-chair' at the senior management table and positions the function as a real generator of value rather than being regarded, as is all too often the case, merely as a cost, and an expensive one at that, which does little more than manage 'pay and rations'. This is a myopic view to take of HR, which should instead be regarded as a means by which organisations can achieve sustainable competitive advantage.

A good starting point

A viable starting point for any organisation is to establish its own Behavioural Competency framework. This will define 'excellence' in terms of behaviour and can provide a common language for many people-related activities across the organisation, e.g. recruitment, performance management etc.

The generic framework described in Chapter 4 is based upon a wide range of studies across organisations, big and small, domestic to the UK and international over the past 25 years. Many organisations have adopted this framework, recognising its relevance to senior management activities and responsibilities. Often, adoption of the generic framework allows an organisation to get 'into the swing' of using behaviours while, in parallel, to start assembling a framework that is specific to it. For instance, subtle inferences are seen in moving from 'Customer Understanding' in the generic framework to 'Client Awareness' in a specific framework, i.e. the competency terminology matches the organisation's own definitional vocabulary, its culture, values and business drivers. This is not playing at semantics but is an acutely important factor to address in order to win acceptance to the concept of the framework by everyone in the organisation. Failure to do will cause confusion.

A typical process for constructing an organisation-specific framework involves a structured study across the organisation, which involves many individuals being interviewed to identify the behaviours that are exhibited across the business. Focus Groups provide additional information concerning future issues, leadership style, culture and climate. This information is distilled to produce the following:

1. A broad-based behavioural framework that defines a comprehensive array of behaviours, clustered into the four key behavioural domains of Thinking, Influencing, Achieving and Self-managing, which will be adopted throughout the organisation.

2. Association of certain behaviours to specific roles.

3. Association of certain behaviours to specific levels.

4. A plan to deliver a broad-ranging communication process to develop awareness and gain commitment from all organisational members ahead of implementing the framework in the four HR areas mentioned above.

From Case Study 10, which considered developing an organisation-specific Behavioural Competency Framework, Figure 8.1 shows an extract from it. As can be seen, this highlights the functional, distinguishing competencies that have been defined for two different levels within the organisation.

Roles to which competencies apply	Competencies for role				Comments
	Thinking	**Engagement**	**Achievement**	**Self Management**	
Core roles	Client Thinking	Engagement	Results Delivery	Disciplined	These competencies are for the core 'transactional' roles
	Analytical Thinking	Client Influencing	Information Probing	Persistence	
Complex roles	Conceptual Thinking	Relationship Management	Innovativeness	Learning Orientation	These additional competencies are for the more 'complex' roles

Figure 8.1

Using competencies in recruitment and selection

Assessing behavioural competencies within the recruitment and selection process is the most effective means by which it can be ensured that new entrants into the organisation, together with internal promotions, will be more likely to deliver the defined behavioural requirements set out in the organisation's competency framework. Other writers may not concur, although in my experience and that of clients with whom my colleagues and I have worked, their method of approach is far less reliable and accurately predictive than will now be outlined.

Having established a clear understanding of the specific competencies that relate to particular roles and levels within the organisation, including setting out what the behaviours actually look like in terms of these roles (which is needed for advertisements and job descriptions), the organisation needs to build its capacity and capability to conduct interviews that will assess applicants' strengths in the required competencies.

The 'competency interview' is only one component of a rigorous selection approach, e.g. Assessment Centres (comprising elements such as behavioural simulation, presentations, business games, psychometric tests, etc.), but it is the step on which greatest dependence should be placed. Clearly, there will be a range of experiences and particular technical skills and knowledge that are required. However, it must be remembered that these attributes represent only threshold performance characteristics. A recruitment process is trying to assess the probability of applicants being able to perform in a role different from that which they currently occupy. Often this new role is at a higher level in an organisation. The critical test, therefore, is to assess their current behavioural competence: remember, we do not want to recruit for 'personality'; instead we want to recruit against actual behaviours. Seeing demonstrable evidence that an individual has learnt to deliver effectively a range of behaviours provides good predictive data that he will similarly learn to deliver other 'higher order' behaviours, e.g. Strategic Thinking, associated with the new role. Using a method that can elicit and measure such data is essential. In our approach, it brings together the recruiting line manager and HR team to work in a strongly collaborative manner, assuming collective responsibility for their decisions.

In our experience, recruitment and selection decisions are often 'off-beam' because any behavioural assessment is limited to how people perform in the interview or the overall recruitment process, in spite of this being an entirely false environment bearing little or no resemblance to what life will be like in the job itself.

What we really want to know is how the individual will behave in the job itself. One of the most powerful predictors of future performance is previous performance and it is this which our interview process explores. Thus, the interview attempts to measure what a person has done previously rather than limit its scope to measuring behaviour in just the interview.

Our method of Competency Based Interviewing (CBI) achieves this and in a very specific way. Our approach asks individuals to describe broad-based achievements in terms of explaining the detail of what they actually did, said, and thought throughout the particular achievement. The interview questioning is generally very open-ended, so encourages individuals to talk about a sequence of events that resulted in a specific outcome. This is very different from providing a tactical example to illustrate a particular behaviour, e.g. "Tell me about when you have planned an acquisition" or "Explain how you have dealt with a rude and abusive customer" or "How have you handled a difficult meeting with major investors?"

When conducting the CBI, interviewers need to encourage the individual to talk about what he has achieved and how. They need to 'uncover' evidence that supports delivery of the behaviours that have been included as requirements in the organisation's job definition. The gathered data needs to satisfy certain criteria in order for it to be considered. For instance, the evidence needs to be volunteered rather than provided in response to a leading question. Such data is not evidencing 'characteristic behaviour' which, of course, lies at the nub of the definition of a competency.

Other 'rules of evidence' include ensuring the data relates to the person concerned and not someone else or gets lost in talking in terms of 'we'. While they may appear very 'teamy', it doesn't accurately discern who did what.

Astute probing by the interviewer provides the necessary level of detail, which we know to be enormously difficult to provide within this method of interview process. Where individuals try to fabricate a story, they will tend to 'clam-up' or demonstrate certain non-verbal signals. (While somewhat 'tongue-in-cheek', if someone is able to do this, perhaps they merit a job anyway because it is quite an accomplishment!)

In our experience, providing we contain a natural human tendency to seek evidence relating to matters about which we are not strictly interested and, thereby, approach the interview in a rigorous and disciplined manner, we can be strongly confident that our judgements are based on reliable and valid data.

We have carried out extensive training of managers in terms of CBI techniques around the globe. From this experience, we are firmly of the belief that it is an entirely feasible proposition to train both line managers and HR professionals to conduct this particular style of interview. Indeed, we would tend to advocate that the most appropriate interviewer is an individual from a line management background rather than HR because they (should) understand the job in depth. Furthermore, it is difficult to recognise the strength of delivery of a competency in a particular context unless that context is understood.

For instance, across the different levels within an organisation, certain competency clusters will be more heavily 'weighted' in terms of their contribution to effective performance. This approach to competency and performance management is illustrated in Figure 8.2.

Competency and role

Figure 8.2

In a role more concerned with establishing future direction, the Thinking competencies play a greater role and, where this also necessitates a significant degree of people management responsibility, the Influencing competencies are equally critical. However, in roles that are more tactical or operational in nature, it is the Achieving competencies that are most significant. Therefore, it is more important that the CBI interviewer is practically cognisant of the required behaviours than, perhaps, the technical skills, which can be assessed through another interview method.

In support of CBI, I do encourage other selection processes, e.g. psychometric tests, to be used. However, I believe that in order to weave the usage of behavioural competencies into the fabric of the organisation, taking a structured approach to training (all) managers to be proficient in conducting this style of interviewing represents a superb starting point. It is abundantly clear that the organisation is taking matters seriously by setting in place a process that represents the most significant hurdle to entry or promotion, i.e. if you can't demonstrate that you deliver the required behaviours, you're not coming in! If you can, welcome!!

Developing competency within a performance management context

Another very significant application of competency implementation occurs when organisations integrate it into their performance management process. Utilising competencies within a performance management context enables managers and their reports to operate a really meaningful and effective coaching process between them. Critically, it is a key means by which the strategic aspirations of an organisation can be cascaded down through the organisation's hierarchy, so helping individuals appreciate the link between what they are asked to do, i.e. their goals and objectives, and those corporate aims. In other words, it enhances Clarity.

From the perspective of wanting to upgrade performance, knowing how delivering a competency will affect the effectiveness by which a particular task is carried out successfully and, thereby, its contribution to achieving an objective or outcome is immensely useful to both manager and individual team member. Figure 8.3 illustrates these connections.

A Leadership Framework for Development

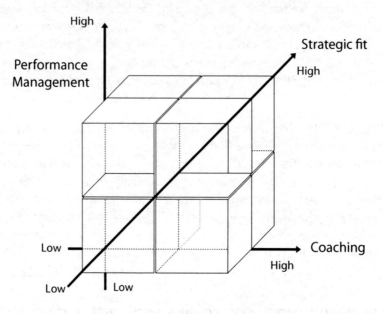

Figure 8.3

- In terms of high levels of Coaching ability but low levels of Performance Management and Strategic Fit, the manager's likely approach is to deliver a satisfying and effective set of interactions with the individual. However, they would not be aligned to the performance needs of the organisation in the short- or medium-term, nor will they be aligned to the organisation's long-term intent.

- On the other hand, if a manager delivers high levels of behaviour in each of the three domains then an effective Coaching and Development approach that is congruent with the business' long-term aims will occur.

Using competency in a learning and development context

A third critical method to utilise competency lies within the learning and development process. As remarked in an earlier chapter, very often a high performer in an operational context performs less adequately when appointed to a broader-based role that considers the future trajectory of the organisation. The need within the performance management process to provide opportunity for development, i.e. to have the chance to practise, say, Conceptual Thinking or to benchmark other organisations in order to enhance their Concern for Excellence behaviour, is vital. Performance management must embrace development goals.

Furthermore, it is sobering to bear in mind that in the vast bulk of studies we have conducted, it is the two developmental competencies, i.e. Developing Others and Self-development, which contribute a very significant differential between outstanding and average performance. Incongruously, many organisations invest large amounts of money into training and development that underpins skills and knowledge but not behaviours. Whilst I would not in any way dissuade an organisation from doing this because skills need to be kept sharp and be updated to reflect, say, technological progression, I would strongly advocate competency development as the learning approach that provides the most efficient return on investment. As I have mentioned frequently throughout the preceding chapters, a leader who is both skilled and behaviourally competent will excel in performance over and above one who is stronger in one dimension only: see Figure 8.4.

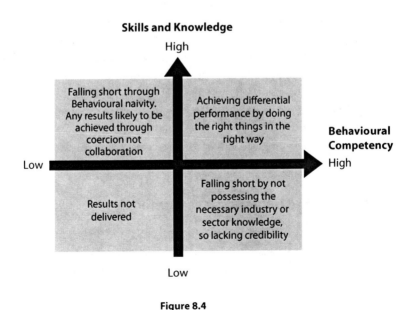

Figure 8.4

To embed reliance upon competencies into an organisation's day-to-day managerial practices, our approach in the field of learning and development concerns providing a safe environment in which individuals can learn to understand and identify what effective delivery of specific competencies looks like and to provide feedback and coaching input to enable people to raise their game so they deliver specific competencies better. Admittedly, this sounds extremely challenging and, perhaps, bordering too closely upon psychological analysis. However, in all our experiences, while there has to be some 'dry' intellectual, explanatory input, once a workshop is released into practice mode, the learning curve, although steep, is climbed quickly.

Developing the Thinking competencies

In the majority of our research and client experience, the competencies in which most managers are weak are Strategic Thinking, Conceptual Thinking and Customer Understanding. Often I have found that due to low Self-development, managers are not especially widely read so their 'train of thought', is relatively narrow. Getting managers to expand their reading coupled with broadening and deepening their networking, i.e. Relationship Building, can provide some very strong foundations on which to build these three critical, cognitive competencies.

In a more formal sense, one developmental approach helps managers to acquire a more strategic orientation when thinking about their organisation. Our coaching methodology in this domain provides individuals with the opportunity to engage in activities that allow them to consider practical applications of these behaviours in the areas for which they are accountable. Remember that when discussing competencies in Chapter 4, I remarked that all too often competencies are not delivered because the organisational culture doesn't provide the requisite opportunity to do so. This is very much more the case with these particular competencies. Of course, for those who are more Radical by Predisposition, they may find it easier to 'release' these behaviours than someone who is more Incremental. Full account is taken of these 'start points' when setting each individual's development programme.

Developing the Influencing competencies

There is no shortage of influencing skill courses and training programs in the market place. Some are born from comprehensive academic research; others appear to have little heritage with research so, in our mind, lack rigour, reliability and validity. Our work in this area is drawn from various research sources[50].

Applying these authors' considerations to our own research and client work over the years, we have developed a programme called 'Engagement through Leadership Skills' (ETLS™). This programme is heavily practice-orientated and rests on the platform of a simple model, which relates to the Behavioural Approaches explained in Chapter 3.

In essence, we have created a simple two-by-two behavioural framework. This can be used practically to help individuals build their influencing and leadership skills. We call this our Engagement Behaviours framework and it is drawn entirely from the leadership behaviours model described in Chapter 3. From that framework, we have combined the leadership behaviours of Democratic and Engaging. A high score in these would indicate an individual to possess a *concern for others*, while a low score would infer *indifference*. Hence the scale: 'Indifference to Others' versus 'Concern for Others'.

Additionally, we have combined the behavioural approaches of Directional, Constructive, Positional and Developmental which, when delivered collectively to a high level, reflect behaviour that provides *focus* and *direction* for others. When scored low, however, it would infer a more *passive, non-directional* or *compliant* mode of behaviour. Hence, in this instance, the second scale of the framework is labelled 'Directive' versus 'Passive'.

The resultant two-dimensional behavioural model maintains an aesthetic congruence with our Predisposition feedback models. See Figure 8.5.

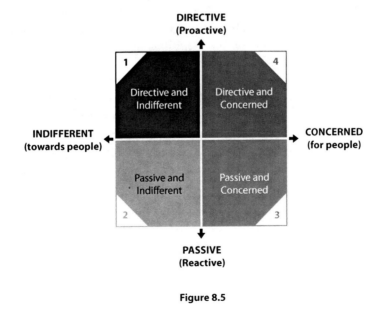

Figure 8.5

Each quadrant formed by the two dimensional axes represents a 'style' of engagement. Simply and straight-forwardly, we posit that the top-right quadrant represents the most effective means of influencing; the other styles will not achieve the same degree of success.

- The top-left quadrant suggests someone who is directional and indifferent. These people are tough 'task-masters' who coercively impose on others and don't care about their sentiments and feelings. We might label this style of engagement as 'The Autocrat', or one of 'fight'.

- The bottom-left quadrant reflects someone who is Passive, rather than Directive, but is still Indifferent. This indicates a person who is reluctant to 'open up' and surface the issues that actually need to be addressed; these individuals suppress the willingness to do so even though they may feel angry about a given situation. We could label this style of engagement as 'The Avoider', or one of 'flight'. (When the Avoider does tackle an issue, it is often after an explosive outburst, i.e. they shift from flight to fight.)

- The bottom-right quadrant indicates someone who is Passive and Concerned. His engagement style is to use friendliness to avoid addressing an awkward issue; he makes light of things. We can label this style of engagement as 'The Companion', or of 'fun'.

  Potentially, this person might not be taken seriously, so when delivering the Engaging behaviour (within the Integrated Framework) it is not especially helpful because he is too engaging, i.e. effusively friendly by not giving due consideration to the (business) matter in hand.

- The top-right quadrant concerns individuals who are both Directional and Concerned. Some years ago this would have attracted the epithet of being 'firm but fair'. We call this engagement style 'The Leader'; it is one of 'focus'. Essentially, it wraps up much of our thinking about the role of the leader, i.e. to set a future ambition for the organisation and to galvanise the collaborative support of others to make his vision into reality.

The best so-and-so I ever worked for

A colleague's father was a senior police officer in Liverpool. Shortly after his father died, my colleague was involved in serving a customer at the branch of the bank where he worked. This customer was a very senior police officer now working in the constabulary where the branch was based. He said he knew an officer in Liverpool with the same surname as my colleague; this turned out to be my colleague's Dad. The customer remarked the following commentary:

"I have only reached my rank by virtue of your father's manner towards me. When I joined the Liverpool police force in the late 1950s, I reported to a sergeant who tossed my first few arrest reports into the bin and shouted at me for producing such poor quality work. He threatened me with dismissal if I didn't improve. Fortunately, I had a change of shift and started reporting to your Dad. I submitted my first arrest report and he read it through and asked me to come to the canteen for a mug of tea. He explained to me what was required in an arrest report and what I needed to do to improve my submissions. We did this each night for the next couple of weeks. Another change of shift ensued and I went back to reporting to the original sergeant. He didn't throw my reports into the bin."

"As I progressed, I had further occasions to work with your father. He was very direct in his manner; you knew where you stood, but he was always genuinely compassionate and caring towards me. He wanted me to get on and succeed. Indeed, if you don't mind me saying so, he was the best f****** b****** I ever worked for." (Maybe that should have been the sub-title for this book?!)

Perhaps this is a somewhat crude and profane way of describing what we mean by this behaviour but this accolade has always inspired my colleague in his leadership career and, indeed, the many people with whom it has been shared over the years.

To expand upon the point made in the paragraph preceding Figure 8.5, this framework helps develop all of the Influencing behaviours. While it is more apparent how, for instance, Inter-personal Awareness and Concern for Impact can be enhanced by considering the framework, it is highly effective in helping leaders manage their Developing Others behaviour by providing a means by which they can deliver relevant, critical and constructive feedback. The framework also helps support development of some of the Self-Managing competencies - for instance Independence, by giving people a proven approach by which they can raise difficult issues, even with a hoary, autocratic boss. For those who are already strong in their Thinking competencies but weaker in the 'people domain', the framework provides a powerful bridge to enable them to enhance their communication and engagement effectiveness. As for 'achieving through others', i.e. Results Focus behaviour, which sits at the very heart of a leader's responsibility, the framework's core philosophy couldn't be more clear and distinct.

In terms of the Integrated Framework, any improvement in an individual's engagement style will have a positive impact upon the effectiveness of the Climate he creates. A fully engaged workforce, working towards the organisation's overarching goals, is the most tangible representation of great Climate.

GPI™ and GMI are introduced into the ETLS™ programme as they help individuals understand the extent of their development journey, particularly in terms of their data concerning Communication and Inter-personal Style, Feelings and Self-Control, and their need for Esteem and Relationships.

- Consider an individual who is highly Collectivist. What does he need to do to be more Directive?

- Consider an individual who is highly Individualist. What does he need to do to be more Concerned?

- What does the predispositionally Impulsive individual need to do to be more systematic in his approach?

- What does the individual highly motivated by Esteem and Relationships need to do to avoid being either an Avoider or a Companion?

In addition to providing the GPI™ and GMI, data outputs from a comprehensive 360° survey process are shared. These enable individual participants to measure their behaviour prior to the training programme, which can be easily re-assessed at particular points in time following the event in order to track developmental impact and progress.

Our aim is to have participants deliver the Engagement Style of the 'Leader' 80% of the time within six months of their participating in an ETLS™ workshop. Utopian idealists might suggest the goal should be 100% delivery, but, realistically, that is impractical. For instance, something may occur which 'offends' an individual's personal values and causes a reaction of 'flight or fight'.

Upping the game in terms of influencing behaviour is absolutely vital for an effective leader, especially those operating in very senior roles. They have a massive and varied stakeholder constituency with which they must continually engage. They need to be able to deliver a consistent message that outlines their vision and strategic aims but in a manner that will win the hearts and minds of each group of stakeholders. If they fail to communicate effectively, rather than achieving a convergence of minds, all that will happen is that these different groups will have divergent views of what is to be done and why. If you wish, no sense of 'true north' prevails.

Achieving

At the heart of any achievement sit some clear goals and objectives and people having clear understanding of their accountabilities and how these relate to each other. Often, however, we see organisations, notably teams of senior managers, struggling to achieve this initial outcome. To help them overcome this crucial stumbling block, the 'Direction-Setting Workshop' has been devised in which teams undertake a number of critical exercises:

- They determine their purpose.

- They identify and rank by importance and severity the issues with which they have to deal. A variety of tools and techniques help them through this assessment. The resultant outcome is a series of Critical Success Factors which, of course, sit at the head of the Integrated Framework.

- They review their Predispositions and Motivations. What natural capabilities exist to begin work towards achieving the Critical Success Factors?

- They set out a clear action plan that establishes accountabilities, responsibilities, deadlines and review points.

Talent management/succession

For many years, it has been well accepted that you don't promote people solely on the basis of performance in the job although, having said that, it is increasingly less likely that poor performers will get promoted as organisations become more meritocratic, i.e. they demonstrate a higher Recognition score within Climate. In my experience, it seemed at one time that people were promoted to the point where their natural Predispositions eventually caught them out. This often led, sadly, to the demise of enterprises.

However, the key point I am making is that if you are going to position someone on a rapid, progressive career track you need to be certain that the individual has the inherent capability and potential to progress at that momentum and, when they attain a senior role, that they will deliver upon their potential of outstanding performance. Furthermore, the right motivational profile is also a pre-requisite.

We have worked with a wide range of organisations around the world using our Development of Potential (DOP™) process. This process assesses individuals against an impressively high-level international benchmark of behavioural capability comprising some 6,000 managers over 25 years. While assessing current capability, more importantly, we are trying to predict the potential for someone to operate at a more senior level.

The DOP™ process

DOP™ consists of an in-depth interview methodology, where individuals recount in detail their career history, starting with an initial sense of responsibility they encountered during adolescence, e.g. school sports team captaincy, part-time job etc. They also relate detailed explanations of several recent (during the last two to three years) significant achievements.

The interview process typically takes at least half a day and enables us to establish a valid assessment of current competency and to estimate the line of potential and development needs of the individual. We are able to assess the extent to which the individual is likely to succeed in a role two or three levels above where he currently operates and, on this basis, establish the range of potential for the individual in question.

Using this methodology, we can assess both the extent of current competency delivery together with the predicted future potential in terms of increasingly more complex roles than that which the individual currently occupies. By also considering core, technical skills, as well as numeracy, verbal reasoning and critical thinking, a clearly defined and comprehensive development agenda can be established for each individual. When this is discussed with his line manager, it permits the manager to agree a 'contract' in terms of funding a particular development and the expected pay-back in terms of improved performance contribution. While this may sound unduly harsh, it is really only another representation of the long-standing theory concerning the 'psychological contract'[51]. The discussion between the individual and his boss also considers how the development can help position the individual for the next role or, potentially, to agree and accept that he has reached a career ceiling or needs to move to another organisation in order to acquire new experience.

This clearly has powerful application in a wide range of situations but none more so when considering individual appointments at the most senior levels. For example, it seems currently that the right of succession to CEO roles in major organisations rests with the Chief Financial Officer or Chief Operating Officer. Behaviourally, the transition from both these roles into that of a CEO represents a huge step and preparation cannot be completed overnight. Using DOP™ allows an initial assessment of whether the individual has the potential to 'bridge the chasm' and to start their development early on. The same would apply to an individual who has recently become a CEO but wishes to progress to a more substantial organisation. Going from heading a £50m organisation to a £500m organisation is no baby-step; heading a FTSE-100 business or major public utility to being the head of one of the world's top 25 organisations are worlds apart in terms of behavioural needs.

Another situation concerns an organisation coming out of a turn-round situation. The CEO who gets an enterprise 'out-of-the-mire' should not necessarily be the 'shoo-in' for continuing in the role in a more growth-orientated situation. DOP™ has proven highly effective in helping organisations manage what are very sensitive situations. The CEO may feel that he has earned the right to continue his stewardship. However, the very behaviours he exercised to sort out the crisis are not usually the ones required to drive growth.

Using DOP™ in this type of approach adds significant value to the talent management process and provides an organisation with a far more robust mechanism in order to ensure continuing success.

More specifically for the CEO, our interview in the DOP™ seeks to elicit the processes in which they have been engaged, e.g. balance sheet management, mergers and acquisitions, multi-currency financials, extent of variety of stakeholders to manager, and the levels at which they have performed, e.g. national or international businesses, simple or complex business models, extent of political influence. Thus the process examines three co-ordinates in which the potential CEO or individual aspiring to become CEO of a more significant enterprise needs to demonstrate his capability. The Chair and Board can then make a judgement call about the 'risk' of any gaps and the means by which these can be closed, either through development or the compensation afforded by other members of the Executive who may score more highly in those particular areas.

Conclusions

In this Chapter, I have set out the means by which the application of competencies can be fully woven into the fabric of an organisation's operational practices. In so doing, it provides the means by which one of the three change levers of Climate can be given a massive impetus. As a result of taking this approach, organisations are seen to move quickly to effect changes to the way they manage vital processes and assemble themselves through their structural design.

Taking any or all of these suggested approaches does not result in an 'overnight change'. These are not 'pixie-dust' solutions. They entail focused effort and application by the organisation's senior managers, which must then cascade down throughout the enterprise. In many instances, I should add, the 'germ of change' has started in a particular business unit within a larger organisation. Its impact has been so significant that it has not gone unnoticed by the most senior leaders who 'catch the virus' and go on to infect the wider organisation to massive effect. In one large group, as a result of working with a particular business unit, the CEO described that business unit as its 'jewel in the crown' and made it clear that he wanted a quick contagion to occur across the wider business.

I have, deliberately, been vague about the organisations that my colleagues and I have worked with. In our experience, trotting out the names of X, Y, or Z looks impressive but tends to mask what is often rather superficial interventions that produce a reverse 'J curve' output, i.e. there is a short-term uplift but this is not sustained.

Developing the ability to consciously deliver excellence across the range of behaviours we have described takes time, perhaps 18 months or so. What we do, therefore, represents a long-term investment but one on which the potential returns over a three to five year window are very considerable.

CHAPTER 9:

Summing it all up

The title of this book adapts the critical theme of Bill Clinton's presidential campaign in 1992, where a sign hung in campaign headquarters by lead political strategist, James Carville, said "It's the economy, stupid!" This provided sharp focus on the key issue that was considered to be foremost in voters' minds.

Likewise, I believe that it is behaviour in organisations by real people, which truly counts as the fundamental driver of organisational success. Behaviour, firstly, in terms of what managers and leaders actually do because they drive and create the enterprise's Climate in terms of what it feels like to work there. Secondly, this feeling, or Climate, drives the behaviour of all employees and results in the delivery of high performance. It has been the issue of behaviour that has formed the fundamental basis of this book.

This final chapter provides a summary of the key points from each of the preceding chapters.

Chapter 1 examined the idea of organisational performance from the perspective of profit and non-profit organisations together with considering what high performance means to a range of different constituents involved with the organisation. These include teams, employees, shareholders, Boards of Governors and other general stakeholders. The key conclusions were:

- Performance represents the intended outcomes the organisation is trying to achieve.

- Performance outcomes vary according to the type of organisation and stakeholders' expectations.

- Performance expectations influence the type of qualities and characteristics needed in people.

- In the main, every organisational member is motivated to deliver the best to help the organisation achieve its performance intentions.

- Irrespective of what the performance expectations may be, senior managers' paramount responsibility is to ensure that the right conditions are in place that enable people to deliver to their best.

- People in an organisation need to understand its purpose and associated objectives and how they tangibly contribute to its achievement.

Chapter 2 introduced the idea of the concept of Organisational Climate. This was defined as 'what it feels like' to work in an organisation and was shown to be the true differentiator of performance. All things being equal, a high-performing organisation will have a measurably superior Climate than a low performing organisation. Furthermore, if Climate is improved, performance will do likewise. Climate represents the condition senior management needs to create an order for an organisation to perform to its optimum. In summary, the key points are:

- Climate is defined as 'what it feels like to work here'.

- Climate concerns people; culture is more concerned with 'how things are done', i.e. rules and procedures. Culture programmes fail because they do not adequately consider the organisation's people.

- Climate differentiates outstanding performing organisations and teams from average and mediocre performing ones.

- Improve your Climate and increase your bottom-line, however that is measured.

- Creating a performance-orientated Climate is the ultimate responsibility for all managers and leaders at all levels of organisational activity.

Chapter 3 considered what needs to be done to create an effective Organisational Climate. The Integrated Framework was presented, which showed that Climate is driven and strongly influenced by three 'change levers', namely the leaders' behavioural approaches, the efficacy of the organisation's design and the effectiveness by which key processes are managed. These three factors represent the 'leadership dynamic', which drives the Climate. If this dynamic is well managed, the right conditions are created in which people can prosper (financially and developmentally), deliver their personal goals and objectives and contribute to the organisation's competitive success.

- The three change levers of structure, behaviours and processes drive Climate.

- Effectively managing these levers represents the ultimate responsibility of the manager or leader and provides the most significant means by which they influence their organisation's performance.

- Numerous case studies show unequivocally that improving how the 'change levers' are managed drives an uplift in Climate and, thereby, an organisation's overall performance in terms of bottom-line, sales, service, product development, staff turnover, innovation.

- Climate and the 'change levers' can all be measured and benchmarked against an international database to provide managers with a highly valid audit of their organisation's relative performance.

- This benchmark audit provides a powerful 'call to action' for senior leaders to establish a strategic change agenda that will precipitate performance improvement across the entire organisation.

Chapter 4 focused on the issue of what drives outstanding leadership performance. The idea of behavioural competency was positioned as the critical differentiator. Over many years of research with numerous occupational groups and at many organisation levels, behaviour has been shown to account for the difference between an outstanding and average performer. Behavioural competencies are shown as the critical features that leaders and managers need to possess in order for them to contribute successfully to the 'leadership dynamic' described through Chapters 2 and 3. Measuring and assessing competencies should form the pivotal decision in recruitment processes; they should contribute the main arbiter in talent management, performance management and succession planning. They can, and should, also form the platform on which an organisation bases its learning and development curriculum. People can succeed in learning to improve the quality and effectiveness in which they deliver behavioural competencies. This learning takes time but, once embedded, the practice is sustainable.

- Competencies are behaviours. They do not concern skills or personality characteristics.

- Extensive research shows that outstanding performance is statistically correlated with an individual possessing and delivering the appropriate behavioural competencies for the situation in which they are engaged. Where a situation doesn't permit delivery, performance will be less effective.

- Behavioural competencies are measurable and assessable. They can be applied across the HR cycle in selection, recruitment, performance management etc.

- When an organisation homes in on developing behaviours, its people's performance rises significantly.

- Enhanced competency delivery results in more effective management of the 'leadership dynamic'.

- Excellent behavioural delivery by managers and leaders creates the right conditions to enable the organisation's broader population to lift its behavioural game. Climate will improve, so will performance.

- Helping people develop their behavioural competencies provides a great opportunity for them to achieve their full career potential.

Chapter 5 introduced the idea of Predispositions, which were defined as representing an individual's natural characteristics. These are differentiated from delivered behaviours, which represent what people actually do. More often than not, jobs throw up situations that require different behaviours to be delivered than those that represent our character or personality. For instance, naturally reserved types will need to overcome their shyness when their job requires them to engage with others through networking and stakeholder management. Organisations pay for delivered behaviours, not preferred ones.

> **In short, predispositions, or personality, sucks!**
>
> **It's your behaviour, stupid, that counts.**

In terms of management development, the distinction between preferred and delivered behaviours is critical. It enables people to understand why it is that certain required behaviours come easily while others are more difficult to master.

- Predispositions are our natural, personal characteristics.

- Predispositions are not necessarily the same thing as actual, delivered behaviour. In a competency context, behaviour represents what is likely to be required in any given job.

- The Glowinkowski Predisposition Indicator (GPI™) assesses three key factors:

  o Problem Solving and Implementation

  o Communication and Inter-personal Style

  o Feelings and Self-control

- The GPI™ profile provides a powerful measure of an individual's predispositional make-up, which enables a sound understanding to be established about why some behaviours come easily and others do not.

Chapter 6 builds upon the definitional content of Chapter 5 by considering more explicitly the links that can be expected to be observed between an individual's predisposition profile and their behaviour. At a general level, for example, an extrovert by predisposition is generally construed to be likely to exhibit friendly and outgoing behaviour, yet a predisposed extrovert can also come over as more assertive and self-assured in his style. Such patterns or 'profile shapes' were discussed to help build an appreciation for the links and associations between natural character and others' perception of what is delivered.

A second set of connections was made between predisposition profiles and the leadership approaches and behavioural competencies described respectively in Chapters 3 and 4. For example, individuals who are predisposed to be more Radical in their thinking style tend to find the behaviours of Strategic and Conceptual Thinking easier to accomplish. Consideration was made towards individuals who are predisposed to a certain competency type but, for various reasons, don't deliver them, often because the organisation's Climate or Culture is an inhibiting factor.

Motivation was also considered in terms of how certain drivers encourage or discourage individuals to display certain leadership practices. For example, individuals who are not strongly motivated by power tend not to be energised by the opportunity to influence others to adopt their ideas or opinions. As a result, they exhibit poorer levels of the influencing behaviour competencies. Equally, individuals motivated by their own high achievement of task delivery often enjoy delivering the task themselves and consequently find effective delegation difficult to achieve.

- Predisposition profiles help individuals understand their particular style of behaviour.

- Predisposition profiles provide insight into why people are perceived as they are.

- Predispositions and motivations can also be linked to an individual's delivery of specific behavioural competencies and leadership style.

- Predispositions do not always flow through to delivered behaviour because organisational contexts sometime stifle this outlet or the right opportunities might not be made available for individuals to deliver a particular approach, e.g. Initiative is impeded by rules.

- One aspect of development concerns individuals learning what their strengths are and playing to these by choosing an occupation or role where there is a good balance or match between their predispositions and the required behaviours.

- Very few senior positions enable the previous point to be a realistic option. Therefore, a major goal of development is to help people learn to deliver those behaviours that do not necessarily fit with their natural predispositions.

Chapter 7 presented a set of case studies, which build on that described at the end of Chapter 3. All of these case studies represent significant interventions delivered by my colleagues and me over the past 15 years. They provided the opportunity to measure, diagnose and audit organisational situations beforehand, deliver the required change implementation and review and assess the consequential outcome.

Collectively, they demonstrate that if a way can be found to help an individual manager or leader to enhance his behavioural delivery it will result in an improvement in the organisation's Climate. This sets the conditions for an improvement in the behaviour of everyone in the broader organisation, which can result in significant improvement in a wide range of organisational performance outcomes.

These case studies represent a clear depiction of the practicality and relevance of the methodologies I have explained throughout the book, all of which are underpinned by valid research and statistical analysis. I firmly believe that when senior managers commit to their organisations to applying a comprehensive behavioural agenda, it is entirely feasible for the full cadre of that enterprise's leadership community to raise its game. Raising managers' behavioural game generates massive rewards for all organisations. These case studies embody the power of measurement; they reinforce the axiom, "If you can't measure, you can't change it."

Chapter 8 focused on implementation in terms of weaving a behavioural competency-based approach into the fabric of organisational life. The chapter discussed the application of behaviours in terms of selection and recruitment, and the practical value of enabling the management population to become intimately involved in selection processes through using the techniques themselves. Also discussed was behavioural application in performance management and how this can be integrated and become part of an ongoing PM process that helps to establish a 'coaching is for experts' culture. Building on these applications is the use of behaviours in the context of talent management in order to measure, assess and develop the potential that prevails in the organisation. Finally, it is explained how behaviours can be adopted into the broader learning and development processes in order to help individuals develop the quality and effectiveness of their behavioural delivery.

There is no doubt that our best successes have been achieved when the organisation really learns the language of the material and cuts the umbilical cord of dependency upon ongoing external consultancy input. This makes real economic sense.

I have been involved within the field of management and organisational performance development for more than 25 years and have had the greatest of privileges to work with many thousands of managers across the world. This has provided me with the opportunity to observe what really makes the difference in terms of their success, the realisation of their potential and the delivery of their organisation's success.

I think it is a no-brainer – it's the behaviour, stupid!

.

APPENDIX I:

Definitions of components of the integrated framework

CLIMATE

DIMENSIONS	SUB-SCALES	ESSENCE STATEMENT
CLARITY	Long-term direction	Well established long-term direction
	Integration	People's/Groups' activities are well integrated
	Co-ordination	Making progress toward long-term direction
CHALLENGE	Innovation	Encouraged to try new approaches
	Achievement	Stretched with goals that are challenging/realistic
CHANGE ORIENTATION	Motivation	Take action before being directed
	Adaptability	Minimum of unnecessary procedures
	Flexibility	A readiness/enthusiasm for change
AUTONOMY	Independence	Does not always have to check/ask permission
	Accountability	A feeling that the individual can make a difference
	Effort	Prepared to work beyond job remit
RECOGNITION	Reward	Differential relation between reward and performance
	Feedback	Receiving effective feedback
	Value and Appreciation	Feeling of being valued and appreciated
INVOLVEMENT	Commitment	Committed to the teams long-term direction
	Trust	Proud to be part of the team
	Synergy	Whole is greater than the sum of parts

LEADERSHIP BEHAVIOURS

DIMENSIONS	SUB-SCALES	ESSENCE STATEMENT
DIRECTIONAL	Strategic	Creates options for the future
	Long-Term Direction	Establishes long-term direction
	Alignment	Co-ordination/drives activities for delivery
ENGAGING	Commitment	Builds the commitment of others
	Presence	Demonstrates credibility and presence
POSITIONAL	Activity level	Delivers an appropriate level of activity
	Delegatory	Is prepared to delegate
CONSTRUCTIVE	Relationships	Builds open and constructive relationships
	Conflict Management	Does not avoid conflict
DEMOCRATIC	Information Sharing	Openly shares appropriate information
	Consultative	Is prepared to use a consultative approach
	Motivational	Will involve and listen to others
DEVELOPMENTAL	Coaching	Provides feedback and encourages development
	Career Planning	Sees development as a key part of the job
	Developing Performance	Helps people to develop their performance

ORGANISATIONAL STRUCTURE & JOB DESIGN

CATEGORY	DIMENSIONS	ESSENCE STATEMENT
STRUCTURE & ORGANISATION	Organisational Overlaps	Individuals/Departments overlap of activities
	Organisational Gaps	Areas of accountability not picked up
	Structural Flexibility	An overall structure which is flexible/responsive
	Headroom (D)	Too much headroom
	Headroom (C)	Too little headroom
	Customer Orientation	Customer requirements drive organisational structure
	Standards	Standards of performance are defined
JOB CHARACTERISTICS	Job Completeness	A complete job
	Job Significance	A job which has significance
	Job Discretion	A job which enables discretion
	Job Co-Operation	A job which surfaces minimum of conflict
	Job Clarity	The job is well defined
	Job Accountability	Accountability of decision-making is clear
	Job Skill Demand	A job which utilises a broad range of skills
	Intrinsic Feedback	The job itself provides feedback
MOTIVATION and FEELINGS	Qualitative Capacity	Work that may be too difficult
	Quantitative Capacity	Work that provides too much to do
	Job Satisfaction	General satisfaction with the job
	Challenge	A job which provides challenge

TEAM PROCESSES

CATEGORY	DIMENSIONS	ESSENCE STATEMENT
PLANNING	Planning Processes	Planning processes are well established
	Business Planning	Business planning drives activities
	Goals & Objectives	Clear goals and objectives are set
RELATIONSHIPS	Team Communication	Communication within the team
	Organisational Communication	Communication with other teams/organisations
	Openness/Trust	There is trust and people are open with each other
	Supportive Behaviour	People support each other/ group needs come first
TEAM EFFECTIVENESS	Skill Balance	An appropriate blend of skill and experience
	Individual Development	Opportunities for individual development
	Feedback & Review	Team performance is reviewed
PERFORMANCE	Decision-Making	Effective decision-making processes
	Efficiency	Resources are used efficiently
	Co-ordination	Team activities are well co-ordinated

APPENDIX 2:

Summary of correlations within the
Climate-Dimension Matrix

	Clarity	Challenge	Change Orientation	Autonomy	Recognition	Involvement
Structure/Organisation	0.599	0.524	0.561	0.522	0.597	0.603
Job Characteristics	0.559	0.532	0.412	0.541	0.539	0.561
Motivation and Feelings	0.509	0.415	0.438	0.477	0.542	0.533

	Clarity	Challenge	Change Orientation	Autonomy	Recognition	Involvement
Planning	0.771	0.621	0.579	0.601	0.654	0.734
Relationships	0.694	0.632	0.649	0.608	0.618	0.762
Team Effectiveness	0.731	0.648	0.653	0.663	0.724	0.752
Performance	0.705	0.602	0.618	0.585	0.617	0.725

	Clarity	Challenge	Change Orientation	Autonomy	Recognition	Involvement
Directional	0.666	0.581	0.524	0.591	0.611	0.652
Engaging	0.582	0.522	0.489	0.534	0.587	0.607
Positional	0.406	0.424	0.314	0.427	0.454	0.446
Constructive	0.39	0.396	0.365	0.395	0.499	0.429
Democratic	0.393	0.408	0.404	0.452	0.471	0.46
Developmental	0.57	0.503	0.508	0.53	0.685	0.558

APPENDIX 3:

Summary definitions of a sample of behaviours from the generic framework

CONCEPTUAL THINKING

Essence Statement

The individual identifies connections and trends between situations and events; collects and collates complex data from a variety of sources; develops creative solutions that master the wider context (group, regulatory environment, social trends etc).

LEVEL 1

Recognises the wider picture

- Recognises the connections between events and data that are not obviously related

- Recognises how one situation may be affected by another and considers the implications on other projects

- Recognises trends in data or series of events

LEVEL 2

Understands the overall picture

- In building a strategy or vision, brings key pieces of information together from disparate sources

- Stands back from day-to-day and thinks creatively to out-manoeuvre obstacles

- Considers how future needs may differ from what has gone before

- Applies knowledge of past situations/trends as appropriate to new environment and not without questioning their validity

- Identifies the underlying issues in complex situations or problems

- Regards business issues as part of a broad context of economic and social factors at a local, national and international level

LEVEL 3

Creates new approaches for practical application

- Translates theoretical processes/procedures into practical applications

- Translates complex data into simplified models for action

- Understands the importance of differential, competitive advantage and seeks to establish new dynamics

- Generates and tests multiple concepts, hypotheses or explanations for a given situation

INTERPERSONAL AWARENESS

Essence Statement

The individual observes people closely and has a good awareness of others' motives, needs and concerns; thinks through how people will react and is able to anticipate problems impassively.

LEVEL 1

Knowledge of others

- Absorbs relevant facts about others

- Takes the time to listen to and recognise the views of others

- Considers the opinions and beliefs of others neutrally

LEVEL 2

Understanding of others

- Is aware of the thoughts of others

- Has the ability to put self into another's position and recognise their concerns

- Develops understanding about the motivators of others

- Thinks about why people do what they do

LEVEL 3

Intuitiveness and recognition

- Observes and understands the meaning of non-verbal behaviour and comprehends what is being communicated

- Perceives accurately and dispassionately how others will react to situations and changes

- Is intuitive to the needs, motives and values of others whilst maintaining detachment

- Demonstrates an accurate and appropriate evaluation without emotional involvement

- Thinks about another's views in order to appraise their situation or expectations

CONCERN FOR EXCELLENCE

Essence Statement

The individual is never satisfied with the *status quo* and continually pursues excellence and improvement in all aspects of work.

LEVEL 1

Personal quality

- Takes personal responsibility for delivery of excellent work

- Aims to consistently provide top quality service

- Invests time in examining work for errors and omissions

- Aims for 'right first time'

- Drives to exceed defined standards

- Challenges existing methods and quality standards and suggests ideas for improvement

LEVEL 2

Setting and improving standards

- Champions the generation of good, new ideas

- Ensures procedures and quality standards are clearly communicated and actioned

- Establishes Key Performance Measures to ensure that work meets the highest quality standards

- Encourages measures of excellence by setting high personal standards as an example

- Follows through on ideas, progressing and evaluating them

- Seeks further opportunities to improve profitability and efficiency

LEVEL 3

Benchmarking

- Actively seeks exemplary practice in the field

- Fosters a climate of continuous improvement

- Regularly reviews procedures in search of improvement

- Identifies areas where improvement will bring strategic advantage

INDEPENDENCE

Essence Statement

The individual raises important issues in the face of anticipated or actual opposition; stands up for own ideas and is not afraid to express thoughts and feelings to colleagues at all levels.

LEVEL 1

Voices opinions

- Thinks things through independently of others

- Knows own mind

- Does not hesitate to share opinions or speak up

LEVEL 2

Takes issue

- Is prepared to stand alone on issues despite collective opposition

- Tackles difficult issues with people

- Questions established systems, norms and values

LEVEL 3

Stands ground

- Consistently defends a position

- Shows courage of own convictions through action

- Maintains ground even in the face of persistent opposition

APPENDIX 4:

An exercise to help distinguish behaviours from skills and other personal attributes

Competency is the critical component that any jobholder, whether a marketing consultant, a waiter or, indeed, a CEO, possesses within the wider array of factors we have discussed, which produces a superior performance outcome.

Consider two roles with which we expect most people will be familiar: a secretary in an office environment and a barman/barwoman (a bar person) in a pub or bar.

Using the tables provided on the next couple of pages, in the left-hand column list the tasks that you expect people in such jobs would have to undertake. In the middle column, list those behaviours you think will underpin the person's approach in delivering these tasks to a satisfactory level. In the right-hand column, list the individual's behaviours or characteristics that truly represent outstanding performance, and absolutely differentiate the person in question as the most impressive secretary or bar person you have ever known.

The Secretary

Tasks & activities	Behaviour	Outstanding Quality
List the tasks that you expect the secretary to undertake.	List the behaviours that the secretary needs to demonstrate in order to be effective in delivering the task.	What characterised the behaviour of the most outstanding secretary you have known – what made her different?

The Bar Person

Tasks & activities	Behaviour	Outstanding Quality
List the tasks that you expect the bar person to undertake.	List the behaviours that the bar person needs to demonstrate in order to be effective in delivering the task.	What characterised the behaviour of the most outstanding bar person you have known – what made him different?

Suggested answers follow, so don't turn the page if you are doing the exercise!

SUGGESTED ANSWERS

- **The Secretary:** Tasks might include answering the telephone, managing e-mail and post, diary management, making travel arrangements.

  Considering the question, "What does a person need to have as a quality or characteristic behaviour in order to do these tasks effectively?", this might include behaviours such as:

  · 'Attention to detail', i.e. being meticulous about spelling and grammar

  · 'Results Focus', i.e. doing things on time to agreed standards

  · 'Thoroughness', i.e. putting together a business travel itinerary completely

  · 'Assertiveness', i.e. not being 'pushed into' putting meetings in the manager's diary (being a good 'gatekeeper')

  Taking things a stage further by asking, "What are the characteristics of the most outstanding secretary we have ever known?", we might identify behaviours identified such as:

  · 'Interpersonal awareness', i.e. the ability to truly understand the needs and concerns of others

  · 'Conceptual thinking', i.e. the secretary seeing the bigger picture and understanding the links between different issues with which the manager is dealing

  · 'Initiative', i.e. being pro-active and thinking *off her own* bat about new ways of doing things more effectively and introducing such changes into the organisation.

- **The Bar Person:** their tasks are likely to include taking orders, mixing and/or pouring drinks, cleaning, handling money and credit cards, stock management, greeting people, dealing with customers' bad behaviour.

· The sorts of behaviours that underpin some of these tasks may not be different from those required by the Secretary. For instance, the task of taking orders is likely to be underpinned by the behaviour of Accuracy or Attention to Detail. The Bar Person will need to exercise Concern for Impact when greeting customers to make them feel welcome and comfortable. He will also need to show assertive behaviour with a difficult or drunken customer

· The outstanding bar person may have had a range of characteristics that made him outstanding but he certainly would have had a high level of Initiative, which underpinned a marketing or sales idea that he implemented. Indeed, this piece of behaviour with its positive outcome for the bar's business may have convinced you that this person had the potential to become the next bar manager.

Suggested completed tables follow:

The Secretary

Tasks & activities	Behaviour	Outstanding Quality
Diary management	Attention to detail	Has the ability to really understand the detailed needs and requirements of her manager
Arranging travel	Politeness	
Shorthand	Empathy	
Typing	Conscientious	Sees the bigger picture
Greeting visitors	Focused	Always remains calm in a crisis
Making coffee	Organised	
Hosting meetings		
Taking telephone calls		
Communication information		

The Bar Person

Tasks & activities	Behaviour	Outstanding Quality
Takes orders	Is polite	Able to come with new ideas for innovations
Mixes drinks	Listens carefully to customers' requests	Knows when and when not to talk
Greets customers	Has attention to detail	When required can deliver real empathy
Throws out drunks		
Stock-takes	Uses memory techniques	
Maintains stock levels	Checks in order to avoid errors	
Takes money and gives change	Is courteous	
Serves customers		
Cleans the bar		

APPENDIX 5:

References

[1] *What Leaders Really Do* by John Kotter, Harvard Business School Press

[2] *See Motivation and Organisational Climate* by George H. Litwin and Robert A. Stringer, Harvard University

[3] *Capitalism, Socialism and Democracy* by Joseph Schumpter (sometimes spelt Schumpeter), Harper Collins Publishers

[4] *Disruptive Technologies: Catching the Wave* by Joseph L. Bower and Clayton M. Christensen, Harvard Business Review, January to February 1995

[5] *The Competent Manager* by Richard Boyatzis, Wiley Inter-Science

[6] *Field Theory in Social Science; Selected Theoretical* Papers by Kurt Lewin, Harper and Row

[7] *The New York Times Magazine*, September 13, 1970.

[8] *Creative Destruction* by Richard Foster and Sarah Kaplan, Currency

[9] Stern, Stewart &Co. at www.sternstewart.com

[10] Marakon at www.marakon.com

[11] *Managing for Value: It's Not Just About the Numbers* by Philippe Haspeslaugh, Tomo Noda and Fares Boulos, Harvard Business Review, July – August, 2001

[12] *Punished by Rewards* by Alfie Kohn, Houghton Mifflin

[13] *The War on Talent* by Ed Michaels, Helen Handfield-Jones and Beth Axelrod, Harvard Business School Press

[14] Aberdeen Group, *The Product Portfolio Management Benchmark Report*, published at: www.aberdeen.com/summary/report/benchmark/RA_PPM_JmB_3359.asp

[15] *The Balanced Scorecard: Translating Strategy Into Action* by Robert S. Kaplan and David P. Norton, Harvard Business School Press

[16] *The Fifth Discipline Fieldbook: Strategies for Building a Learning Organisation* by Peter Senge, Nicholas Brealey Publishing

[17] *The Fish Rots From The Head: The Crisis in our Boardrooms – Developing the Crucial Skills of the Competent Director* by Bob Garrett, Profile Business. Also, *A Strategic Approach to Corporate Governance and Best Practice in Corporate Governance*, both by Adrian Davies, Gower

[18] *Maverick! The Success Story Behind the World's Most Unusual Workplace* by Ricardo Semler, Random House Business Books

[19] http://www.liverpoolfc.tv/lfc_story/1959.htm

[20] http://www.maslow.com

[21] *One More Time: How Do You Motivate Employees?* by Frederick Herzberg, Harvard Business Review, reprinted January 2003.

[22] *The Developmental Sequence in Small Groups* by Brian Tuckman, published in *The Psychological Bulletin, 63, 384-399.*

[23] *Understanding Customer Expectations of Service* by A Parasuraman, L.L. Berry and V. A. Zeithaml, Sloan Management Review, 39, Spring 1991

[24] *The Service Profit Chain – How Leading Companies Link Profit and Growth to Loyalty, Satisfaction and Value* by James L. Heskett, W. Earl Sasser Jr. and Leonard A. Schlesinger, Free Press

[25] *Strategy and Society: The Link Between Competitive Advantage and Corporate Social Responsibility* by Michael Porter and Mark Kramer, Harvard Business Review, December 2006

[26] www.tomorrowscompany.com

[27] *A Causal Model of Organisational Performance and Change* by W.W. Burke and G.H. Litwin, Journal of Management, 1992, Vol. 18, No.3, 523-545

[28] *The Organisational Culture of Idea-management: a creative climate for the management of ideas* by G. Ekvall, Chapter 7, Managing Innovation, Sage Publications

[29] *The New Leaders: Transforming the Art of Leadership into the Science of Results* by Daniel Goleman, with Ricahrd Boyatzos and Annie McKee, Sphere

[30] *Developing Learning Skills* by Sylvia Downs, referenced at www.positivechargein ternational.com/articles/positivChargeInternational_1.pdf

[31] *Origin of the Species* by Charles Darwin, Gramercy Books

[32] www.valuebasedmanagement.net/methods_beckhard_change_model.html

[33] *Failure to escape traumatic shock* by Martin Seligman and Steve Maier, *Journal of Experimental Psychology*, 74, 1-9, also *Science and Human Behaviour* by B.F. Skinner, The Free Press

[34] See 16, also *Organizational Learning: A theory of action perspective*, and *Organizational Learning II: Theory, method and practice* both by Chris Argyris and Donald Schön, Addison Wesley

[35] *The Wealth of Nations: Inquiry into the Nature and Causes of the Wealth of Nations* by Adam Smith, Hackett Publishing Co., Inc.

[36] As per 5

[37] *The Art of Possibility* by Benjamin Zander, Harvard Business School Press

[38] *An Introduction to the Five-Factor Model and Its Applications* by Robert R. McCrae and Oliver P. John. (This is an article available as public domain information, as a result of it relating to research funded by the federal US government.)

[39] *Scientific Analysis* by Raymond Cattell, Aldine; *A Model for Personality* by Hans Eynsenck, Springer-Verlag; *Human Motivation* by David McClelland, Cambridge University Press. (For Boyatzis see reference 5; for Lewin see reference 6.)

[40] *Winnie the Pooh: Complete Collection of Stories and Poems* by A.A. Milne, illustrated by E.H. Shepard, Methuen Winnie The Pooh

[41] *Psychopathy, machiavellianism, and narcissism in the Five-Factor model and the HEXACO model of personality structure* by K. Lee and M.C. Ashton, *Personality and Individual Differences, 38*, 1571-1582

[42] www.institute21.stanford.edu/summer/speakers/prime_reading.html

[43] *Explorations in Personality* by H. A. Murray (Charles), OUP USA

[44] *The Three Musketeers* by Alexandre Dumas, Penguin

[45] See reference 34, also *Theory in practice: Increasing professional effectiveness* by Chris Argyris and Donald Schön, Jossey-Bass

[46] *A Technique for the Measurement of Attitudes* by Rensis Likert, Archives of Psychology 140 (published 1932)

[47] *Good to Great* by Jim Collins, Random House Business Books

[48] *Field theory in science; selected theoretical papers* by Kurt Lewin, edited by D. Cartwright, published in 1951

49 www.quotedb.com/quotes/1483

50 'Conflict and Conflict Management' by Kenneth Thomas in The Handbook of Industrial and Organisation Psychology, John Wiley & Sons; The Managerial Grid by R.R. Blake and S. Mouton, Gulf Publishing; and www.psychometrics.com/docs/tki%20technical%20brief.pdf

51 Fairness at work and the psychological contract: Issues in People Management and Motivation and the psychological contract: Issues in people management both by D. Guest and N. Conway, IPD; also New Deals by P. Herriot and C. Pemberton, Wiley.